Liberal World Order and Its Critics

Liberals blame the retreat of the liberal world order on populists at home and authoritarian leaders abroad. Only liberalism, so they claim, can defend the rules-based international system against demagogy, corruption and nationalism. This provocative book contends that the liberal world order is illiberal and undemocratic – intolerant about the cultural values of ordinary people in the West and elsewhere while concentrating power in the hands of unaccountable Western elites and Western-dominated institutions.

Under the influence of contemporary liberalism, the international system is fuelling economic injustice, social fragmentation and a worldwide "culture war" between globalists and nativists. Liberals, far from defending rules, have broken international law and imposed their version of market fundamentalism and democracy promotion by military means. Liberal "civilisation" has fuelled resentment across the world by imposing a narrow worldview that pits cultures against one another. To avoid a descent into a violent culture clash, this book proposes radical ideas for international order that take the form of cultural commonwealths – social bonds and cross-border cultural ties on which international trust and cooperation depends. The book's defence of an older order against both liberals and nationalists will speak to all readers trying to understand our age of anger.

This book will be of key interest to scholars, students and readers of liberalism, political theory and democracy, and more broadly to comparative politics and international relations.

Adrian Pabst is Reader in Politics at the School of Politics and International Relations, University of Kent, UK.

World Politics and Dialogues of Civilizations Series

Series Editor: Raffaele Marchetti
LUISS Guido Carli University, Italy

This new series aims to explore alternative models of the social, political and economic developments at regional and world levels in order to advance theoretical understanding, promote political debate, and provide policy-oriented advice. It focuses on six broad macro-areas: policies, institutions, and shared prosperity; infrastructure for global inclusive development; the economy beyond the failure of conventional models; East and West, North and South; civilisations against the threat of social barbarism; life space for humanity.

The series is linked to the research carried out by the Dialogue of Civilizations-DoC Research Institute (Berlin) but is open to external contribution.

Debating Migration to Europe
Welfare vs Identity
Raffaele Marchetti

Liberal World Order and Its Critics
Civilisational States and Cultural Commonwealths
Adrian Pabst

For more information about this series, please visit: www.routledge.com/ World-Politics-and-Dialogues-of-Civilizations/book-series/DOC

Liberal World Order and Its Critics

Civilisational States and Cultural Commonwealths

Adrian Pabst

Routledge
Taylor & Francis Group
LONDON AND NEW YORK

DOC RESEARCH INSTITUTE

First published 2019 by Routledge

2 Park Square, Milton Park, Abingdon, Oxon, OX14 4RN

605 Third Avenue, New York, NY 10017

Routledge is an imprint of the Taylor & Francis Group, an informa business

First issued in paperback 2020

British Library Cataloguing-in-Publication Data
A catalogue record for this book is available from the British Library

Library of Congress Cataloging-in-Publication Data
A catalog record has been requested for this book

ISBN: 978-0-367-02993-7 (hbk)
ISBN: 978-0-367-78812-4 (pbk)

Typeset in Times New Roman
by Deanta Global Publishing Services, Chennai, India

In the intercourse between nations, we are apt to rely too much on the instrumental part. We lay too much weight upon the formality of treaties and compacts. We do not act much more wisely when we trust to the interests of men as guarantees of their engagements. […] Men are not tied to one another by papers and seals. They are led to associate by resemblances, by conformities, by sympathies. It is with nations as with individuals. Nothing is so strong a tie of amity between nation and nation as correspondence in laws, customs, manners, and habits of life. They have more than the force of treaties in themselves. They are obligations written in the heart. They approximate men to men, without their knowledge, and sometimes against their intentions. The secret, unseen, but irrefragable bond of habitual intercourse holds them together even when their perverse and litigious nature sets them to equivocate, scuffle, and fight, about the terms of their written obligations. […] There have been periods of time in which communities, apparently in peace with each other, have been more perfectly separated than, in later times, many nations in Europe have been in the course of long and bloody wars. The cause must be sought in the similitude throughout of religion, laws, and manners. At bottom, these are all the same. The writers on public law have often called this aggregate of nations a Commonwealth. They had reason.

Edmund Burke, *The First Letter on a Regicide Peace* (1796)

Contents

Acknowledgements

This book is the fruit of conversations with friends and colleagues over many years. I would like to thank Will Bain, Richard Beardsworth, Russell Berman, Maxim Bratersky, Alan Cafruny, Tom Casier, Christopher Coker, Matthew Dal Santo, Iain Ferguson, Trine Flockhart, Renato Flores, Maurice Glasman, Paul Grenier, Leonid Grigoryev, Sergey Karaganov, Andrej Krickovic, Anthony F. Lang Jr, Anatol Lieven, Tim Luke, Fyodor Lukyanov, John Mearsheimer, John Milbank, James Noyes, Vassilios Paipais, David Pan, Victoria Pavliushina, Richard Sakwa, Kiron Skinner, Dmitry Suslov, Nandan Unnikrishnan and Xin Zhang, as well as my father Reinhart and my godfather Klaus Wittmann.

I am very grateful to my colleagues of the World Public Forum and the Dialogue of Civilizations Research Institute, in particular Fred Dallmayr, Alexander Dubowy, Piotr Dutkiewicz, Ekaterina Gerus, John Laughland, Grégory Jullien, Raffaele Marchetti, Manuel Montes, Ashis Nandy, Fabio Petito, Vladimir Popov, Alexander Rahr, Peter Schulze, Walter Schwimmer, Jens Wendland and Vladimir Yakunin.

Earlier versions of some of the chapters were presented at various conferences and workshops. Chapter 1 is based on a paper I gave at a conference on "The return of spheres of influence? Continuity and change in geopolitics" at the University of Helsinki on 10 June 2016. Chapter 2 is a much revised version of a paper presented at a workshop on "An emerging new world order? Building blocs, drivers and perspectives" hosted by the Dialogue of Civilizations Research Institute in Berlin on 17 June 2017.

An earlier version of Chapter 3 is a paper that I gave at a conference on "Inventing hegemonies: Theories and approaches" at the University of Warsaw on 21 May 2018. Chapter 4 is based on a paper I delivered at a conference on "The future of Western civilization" at the Hoover Institution, Stanford University on 8 May 2017. I would like to thank the organisers and participants for their comments and suggestions that have helped me to develop my ideas.

Nick Rengger, who died on 16 September 2018, taught me more about international society than anyone else, and it is to him that I dedicate this book.

Introduction

Liberal world order in retreat

The liberal world order that came into existence after the Second World War and expanded at the end of the Cold War is in retreat. Brexit and the election of Donald Trump mark a revolt against the economic and social liberalism that underpins globalisation, mass immigration and multilateral free trade. Trump's victory also casts a shadow over a bipartisan consensus in the US for the past 70 years, which was in favour of the Western security community, multilateral cooperation, international law, democracy promotion and the defence of universal human rights.[1]

Meanwhile, the rise to power of Emmanuel Macron and the survival of Angela Merkel do little to change the fundamental risk of disintegration facing the European Union (EU) and the rollback of liberal democracy in Eastern Europe.[2] Across the West, a new alliance of working-class and lower middle-class voters has risen up against unaccountable elites and remote technocracy. In each case, the economic losers of liberal globalisation have won a rare victory over the Davos oligarchy with its creed of low wages, deindustrialisation, job-exporting trade deals, the deregulation of global finance and endless foreign war.[3]

But at the same time, Brexit and Trumpism are also supported by groups of extreme neo-liberals who reject even the limited international political restraints on capital. They prefer protectionism, nationalism and perhaps war because this allows them to rip up environmental, economic and social protections. In ways that are reminiscent of the 1930s, some capitalists back the authoritarian statism of both the hard left and the radical right in an attempt to shore up their oligarchic power, which further undermines liberal internationalism from within. Something similar is happening in non-Western countries where a hybrid fusion of brutal market competition and tight state control has become normative. The demise of democratisation and the rise of strongmen in countries as diverse as China, India, Russia, Japan and the Philippines pose the most significant threat to the institutions of the liberal world order since the slide into dictatorship during the interwar period.[4]

As part of a wider shift from a values-based foreign policy to an interest-based contest among "Great Powers", the Western-dominated liberal world order since 1989 is unlikely to continue unchanged or disappear altogether. Rather, what may emerge is a "multi-order",[5] whereby the international system with the UN and other international organisations at the apex will endure but also witness a Great Power competition for hegemony. The US-centric and the Sino-Centric order will vie for power and influence, with Russia and India prepared to do deals with whoever shows them greater respect and acknowledges their national interests.

But trans-regional hegemons and rival spheres of influence that are underpinned by competing civilisational visions can clash, and a cultural competition for hegemony is less predictable and possibly even more dangerous than the struggle between sovereign states based on opposing ideologies, as happened during the Cold War. In addition, each bloc is divided: the US-dominated order is split between more liberal-cosmopolitan EU elites and more national-conservative governments in the US and Japan, while the Chinese leadership views many neighbouring countries as little more than vassal states that are culturally inferior – with Russia stuck in a geopolitical grey zone.[6]

The liberal world order, which continues to be at the heart of the international system, is not about to crash. Liberal ideas and institutions are not all bad and many look set to persist. But liberalism cannot escape its own inner contradiction between market anarchy and the technocratic state – thereby fuelling the flames of anger to which one response is populist nationalism.[7] Yet the insurgents are just as elite as the establishment, while many people and their beliefs and values are not represented by any of the old political parties or the new militant movements. The social contract on which the liberal world order rests is fundamentally broken. The downward spiral of "populist demagogy and the fanaticism of the centre"[8] will last as long as liberals fail to recognise the nature of the current crisis. It is neither merely cyclical because it is not just a periodic setback in an otherwise linear history of progress. Neither are we facing the terminal crisis of an entire system that is about to implode. Marx's prophecy of capitalism's collapse has not and likely will not come to pass.

Rather, we are witnessing a new kind of crisis because liberalism erodes the economic and cultural foundations on which it rests, notably the progress of shared prosperity and a shared civic identity upon which both a vibrant market economy and democracy depend. Crucially, the liberal world order is based on the Western political civilisation, which grew out of the 1941 Atlantic Charter and underpinned the international system for 70 years. But this political civilisation with its tendency towards crony capitalism, bureaucratic statism, unfettered globalisation and rampant liberalism has had the effect of undermining the cultural civilisation of the West with its accentuation of socially embedded markets, plural states, a balance between patriotism and internationalism, as well as personalism and the defence of human dignity. Thus, the liberal order threatens the very civilisational branch on which it sits.

This extended essay is divided into four chapters. Chapter 1 provides an account of the rise and fall of the liberal world order since its inception in the early twentieth century, notably its achievements and failures after 1989 but also its wider roots in liberalism's tendency towards a hegemonic sphere of influence and even imperialism. In Chapter 2, the essay offers an analysis of the contemporary backlash against liberalism and its ideological drivers – in particular the failure of liberal progressivism and identity politics but also the rival ideology of nationalist traditionalism, which can be found in Trumpism as well as in the illiberal non-West. Chapter 3 charts the competition for hegemony between rival forces, including the civilisational-states of China and Russia, which are based on a claim to embody unique cultural, ethnic and familial relationships that encompass communities both at home and abroad.

Chapter 4 turns to the idea of cultural commonwealths as an embodiment of human association and an alternative to the liberal focus on individuals, sovereign states, free-trade areas or some form of cosmopolitan world government. As a civilisational and not just a geopolitical community, the wider West – potentially encompassing India and Russia – can not only reverse Western relative decline vis-à-vis China and the "rising rest" but also play a key role in upholding the once and future order of human association. Chapter 5 argues that Western civilisation cannot be reduced to the liberal empire but reflects overlapping cultural commonwealths that emerged from the complex connections between different world civilisations. A richer understanding of Western civilisation not only provides conceptual resources to rethink the West but also to build bridges with other civilisations. Key to such a dialogue of civilisations are two concepts that the chapter develops – covenant and commonwealth. Covenant reflects a sense of belonging across generations around a commitment to mutual flourishing, while commonwealth provides a lens through which to focus on cultural and social ties that can provide a different framework for cooperation within and between nations and peoples.

Notes

1 Robin Niblett, 'Liberalism in Retreat: The Demise of a Dream', *Foreign Affairs*, Vol. 96, no. 1 (Jan.–Feb. 2017), pp. 17–24; G. John Ikenberry, 'The End of the Liberal International Order?', *International Affairs*, Vol. 94, no. 1 (2018), pp. 7–23.

2 Ivan Krastev, *After Europe* (Philadelphia, PA; University of Pennsylvania Press, 2017); Douglas Murray, *The Strange Death of Europe*: *Immigration, Identity, Islam* (London: Bloomsbury, 2017); Jan Zielonka, *Counter-Revolution. Liberal Europe in retreat* (Oxford: Oxford University Press, 2018).
3 Adrian Pabst, 'Brexit, Post-Liberalism, and the Politics of Paradox', *Telos* No. 176 (Fall 2016), pp. 189–201; 'Trump's Triumph: The Failure of Clinton's Progressive Politics and the Demise of the Liberal World Order', *Telos* No. 177 (Winter 2016), pp. 192–197.
4 Bill Emmott, *The Fate of the West. The Battle to Save the World's Most Successful Political Idea* (London: Profile Books, 2017); Edward Luce, *The Retreat of Western Liberalism* (London: Little, Brown, 2017).
5 Trine Flockhart, 'The Coming Multi-Order World', *Contemporary Security Policy*, Vol. 37, no. 1 (2016), pp. 3–30.
6 Richard Sakwa, *Russia against the Rest: The Post-Cold War Crisis of World Order* (Cambridge: Cambridge University Press, 2017).
7 Adrian Pabst, *The Demons of Liberal Democracy* (Cambridge: Polity, 2019).
8 Pierre Manent, 'Démagogie populiste et fanatisme du centre', in Michel Wieviorka (ed.), *Le peuple existe-t-il?* (Auxerre: Sciences Humaines, 2012), pp. 275–286; trans. 'Populist Demagogy and the Fanaticism of the Center', tr. Evelyn Flashner, *American Affairs*, Vol. 1, no. 2 (2017), pp. 9–18.

1   Hubris

The rise and fall of the liberal world order

The liberal world order in question

The beginning of the liberal world order is commonly traced to the post-1945 creation of a new set of multilateral arrangements – from the Bretton Woods institutions (the International Monetary Fund [IMF] and the World Bank) via the United Nations, the Universal Declaration of Human Rights and the Geneva Genocide Convention to the North Atlantic Treaty Organisation (NATO) and later the General Agreement on Tariffs and Trade, which subsequently became the World Trade Organisation (WTO). After two great depressions (1873–1896 and 1929–1932) and two world wars, the aim was to tame the forces of imperialism, nationalism and *laissez-faire* capitalism while at the same time avoiding the totalitarian state corporatism of the communist, fascist and national-socialist regimes. Thus was born the idea of "embedded liberalism", which sought to constrain the sovereign power of national states and regulate the flow of free-roaming global capital.[1]

The 1930s and early 1940s had seen a lethal mix of depression, tyranny, war and genocide. After 1945, the Western world witnessed the creation of a US-led liberal order that consisted in a rules-based system in which cooperation between like-minded countries supplanted inter-state competition, multilateralism replaced the imperial balance of power and commitment to universal values overrode the sole pursuit of national interests. This order rested on the 1941 Atlantic Charter and the US-dominated institutions of Bretton Woods, NATO and GATT/WTO, which gave the US special rights and privileges in exchange for providing security for its allies in Europe and Asia. It created an "international society" of sovereign states that is, in the words of Hedley Bull, more than an unstable balance of power (*contra* realism) but less than a unified world government (*contra* cosmopolitanism).[2]

As one of two super-powers, the US provided not just global public goods such as free trade and freedom of the seas but also an economic and security umbrella for old friends and former foes: loans to the UK (the Marshall

Plan) and the creation of open-ended alliances with Western Europe and Japan. However, as Joseph Nye reminds us, the post-war system of embedded liberalism was limited in scope and success.[3] It was originally confined to the Atlantic part of the world and failed to prevent the Cold War with the USSR that led to the "loss" of China, Soviet expansionism in Central and Eastern Europe, the partition of Germany, a permanent standoff on the Korean peninsula and nuclear brinkmanship involving Turkey and Cuba, as well as the devastating war in Vietnam. Elsewhere, the US-sponsored "free world" included support for dictatorships as well as democracies, and it served US self-interest as much as it served the interests of American allies old and new.

After 1989, liberalism became for some time the dominant ideology, as the "end of history" seemed to herald a global convergence towards Western liberal market democracy as the "final form of human government".[4] First, the former Soviet bloc appeared to abandon totalitarian communism in favour of democratic capitalism, while China and India looked set to replace central planning with the bureaucratic free market. Then Latin America was joined by much of Asia in embracing neo-liberal structural reforms and a gradual integration into the world economy. Bipolarity gave way to unipolarity with the US as the sole superpower now in charge of upholding the new world order and spreading open markets, democracy, the rule of law, individual human rights and elected governments – or so the theory went. Underpinning this order was the belief that open and transparent markets with minimal government intervention, combined with democratic rule, would generate prosperity, peace and partnership.

For some time, this belief seemed to be borne out by evidence. Economic reforms led to the spread of democracy: according to the independent and non-profit organisation Freedom House, the number of market democracies increased from 44 in 1997 to 86 in 2015, and this group of countries accounts for around 70 per cent of global gross domestic product (GDP) and 40 per cent of the world's population.[5] Moreover, liberal values also spread as the order expanded – including the notion that foreign military intervention is legitimate in cases where governments oppress their own populations or destabilise neighbouring countries. This led to the creation of the International Criminal Court in 1998 and the UN vote on enshrining the "Responsibility to Protect" (R2P) that enables foreign governments to intervene in order to prevent atrocities within the borders of a sovereign state. Thus, the liberal world order sought to combine the Westphalian principle of national sovereignty with supposedly universal (but in reality, narrowly Western individualistic) standards of human rights.

Today, the US – even under the administration of President Donald Trump – continues to provide key global public goods based on its economic and military might. Building on the "Washington consensus" in place since the late 1970s, the US Federal Reserve secures some measure of financial stability by acting as a lender of last resort and using the "exorbitant privilege" of the US Dollar that still enjoys the status of the sole world currency.[6] The US Navy patrols worldwide waters to police the law of the seas and defend the freedom of navigation, while the US Army and the Air Force can be deployed from around 750 bases around the globe to protect critical global infrastructure such as access to space and the independent worldwide web. In addition, the NSA has built a global network of surveillance via a complex satellite system. Complementing its hard power is American soft power,[7] such as the most extensive web of embassies, consulates and trade missions, as well as bilateral treaties and the influence of the American "culture industry".

In short, the liberal world order unwritten by the US has set the rules for the entire international community – an interlocking web of values, institutions and relations that makes up the international system and encompasses maritime law, non-proliferation mechanisms, trade deals and financial arrangements.

Yet the Brexit vote and the election of Trump raise fundamental questions about the continuity and resilience of this order in the face of unprecedented opposition from outside and inside the Western world – including the extra-civilisational challenges of Islamic terrorism and the authoritarian rollback of democracy worldwide, as well as the intra-civilisational challenges of economic and cultural insecurity combined with the lack of public trust in the institutions of liberal democracy.[8] These two challenges threaten the foundations of the post-war international system and cast doubt on the ability of liberalism to provide a robust response.

Can the liberal world order endure?

The current crisis of the liberal world order is associated with one (or more) of the following challenges. First of all, there are the costs of upholding the system that may outweigh its benefits for the US and there is a lack of commitment to the foundational values of free trade, open borders and democracy promotion (President Trump's position). Second, at a time when the US seems to be retreating (former President Obama's notion of "leading from behind"), the global power shift towards countries such as China, India and Russia boost those forces that not only contest US leadership and Western values but also build parallel institutions – including the Eurasian Economic Union and the Shanghai Cooperation Organisation. This defies Western norms of liberal governance and represents a rejection of any external interference in support of democracy or human rights. Third, the rise of non-state actors such as multinational corporations or terrorist organisations has the effect of undermining transparent markets, democracies and fundamental freedoms.[9] Fourth, there is deep domestic unease with globalisation and the rise of anti-establishment insurgencies that promise more protection and a greater emphasis on national sovereignty – as encapsulated by the Brexit motto "take back control" and Donald Trump's pledge to "make America great again".

The advocates of the liberal world order contend that the current crisis is but a temporary setback in an otherwise broadly linear history of progress. Their argument is that the ship of globalisation will not be blown off course for long: liberalism and democracy are resilient and can cope with headwinds because liberal institutions adapt to popular concerns and have a better capacity to renew themselves than authoritarian alternatives. The peaceful transfer of powers within democracies between rival parties and candidates is the most effective way of restoring the legitimacy of the political system. Similarly, developed market economies regain momentum thanks to models of growth and distribution of wealth that are consumption- and innovation-driven rather than being as dependent on export and foreign investment as in the case of emerging markets or developing countries.

Crucially, the supporters of liberalism claim that the post-war system endures even at a time when US leadership is weakening and Western moral authority is in crisis. According to G. John Ikenberry, the liberal world order can survive and even thrive precisely because it can accommodate the rising powers.[10] The four reasons Ikenberry gives are, first of all, the low likelihood of a war between the "great powers"; second, the integration of new powers into the liberal world order and its expansion, as evinced by the behaviour of China, India and others; third, the absence of a systemic alternative to the liberal world order; fourth, the general tendency of major states to align themselves with others around shared interests, such as financial stability, nuclear non-proliferation and free trade. In Ikenberry's words, the liberal world order is "is also distinctive in its integrative and expansive character. In essence, it is 'easy to join and hard to overturn'".[11]

Although we are seeing the rise of both old and new "great powers" and multiple pathways to modernity, no grand alternative to dominant liberalism seems to exist.[12] Multipolarity – in the sense of alternative models to Western capitalism or global governance – has failed to materialise as the BRICS (Brazil, Russia, India, China and South Africa) have all adopted variants of capitalism that depend on access to world markets for growth and development. Neither they nor any other emerging powers – so the argument goes – have created blocs, exclusive spheres of influence, or closed geopolitical systems that could rival, never mind replace, the open, rules-based system organised around national state sovereignty and transnational cooperation. While some power and authority might shift from West to East and North to South, liberal domination looks set to last for three reasons given by Michael Cox: first, the US is one of the most powerful countries with a young population and a growing power to innovate, especially in robotics and automation; second, the transatlantic alliance remains the only global military structure capable of projecting power worldwide and deploying military means; third, so far, China is neither able nor willing to replace the US as the sole global super-power, and the "rising rest" want to integrate rather than overthrow the Western liberal order.[13]

China's stunning economic performance since 1989 is part of an accelerated process of catching up with advanced economies, but, so far, the Chinese economy is only about 70 per cent of the size of the US economy, and its population is rapidly ageing, while the relaxing of the one-child policy has until now not produced the hoped-for reversal in the country's demographic fortunes. In addition, Washington spends approximately four times as much on its military as Beijing does, and even the extensive modernisation of China's army and navy will not lead to parity for many years. Although the Chinese leadership is flexing its muscles in relation to the South and East China Sea, it will not be able to push the US out of the Western Pacific, never mind exercise global military hegemony. It is far from clear whether China's model of state capitalism could ever compete with the vibrant innovation culture, buoyant demographics and falling energy costs of the US.

But more fundamentally, the claim is that China has embraced the liberal order precisely because it benefits from it. Further integration with the global economy will sustain the modernising strategy of the governing Communist Party, which is crucial to its survival and hegemony. As the current debate over the future of globalisation and free trade suggests, China under President Xi Jinping appears to be coming to the rescue of a liberal economic system that is under threat from Trump's protectionist vision and the prospect of American mercantilism.[14] In his speech at the World Economic Forum in Davos in January 2017, Xi acknowledged the problems associated with an increasingly global economy but he also defended this model, saying that "globalisation has powered global growth and facilitated movement of goods and capital, advances in science, technology and civilisation, and interactions among people".[15] China seems committed to a version of globalisation and state capitalism that is compatible with economic liberalism, even if Beijing continues to be opposed to political liberalism.

By contrast, Trump promised in his inauguration address that "we must protect our borders from the ravages of other countries making our products, stealing our companies and destroying our jobs. Protection will lead to great prosperity and strength [...] We will follow two simple rules: buy American and hire American".[16] So whereas Trump's policies could undermine liberal globalisation and perhaps even unleash trade wars, Xi appears to support a model that has strengthened both China and the global *status quo*.

As a New York billionaire who rode to fame by perfecting the "art of the deal", Trump might well turn out to exercise political power as a pragmatic businessman rather than a crazed ideologue. The tax cuts and deregulation of Wall St that the Trump administration has implemented shows its commitment to the oligarchy at the heart of the US political system. Trump's promise to increase defence spending and boost the capabilities of the US Navy suggests that he is not about to surrender the Western Pacific to China. His preference for bilateral instead of multilateral trade deals will likely strengthen the bargaining position of the US and yield greater power based on a policy of divide-and-rule. Trump's determination to communicate directly with average Americans via his Twitter tirades might also help him to build domestic majority support for a recalibrated system in which US leadership serves national instead of foreign interests – bombing Syria to assert US influence rather than bringing about democracy. Paradoxically, Trump's illiberal approach could jolt the Western-led liberal world order out of its current complacency and reform it before either descending into anarchy or seeing it replaced by a Sino-centric system.

The defenders of the liberal world order argue just that. While they now disavow the liberal "end of history" thesis, their argument is that liberal democracy and the liberal international order tend to emerge stronger from periods when faced with the dark forces of global politics – including illiberalism, autocracy, nationalism, protectionism, spheres of influence and the revision of borders. But a fundamental evolution is growing international interdependency and liberalism's unique capacity to adapt and provide solutions to the problems of modernity and globalisation. The strength of the liberal tradition is to combine pragmatic adaptability and institutional innovations to new challenges with a principled commitment to the dignity and freedom of the individual and to tolerance of diversity. These principles are reflected in the practices and institutions of the liberal international order, which are far more resilient than critics of liberalism recognise because they serve the most important interests of its members – hence the appeal of the liberal world order to governments that are neither liberal nor democratic.

However, this reasoning rests on two assumptions that are little more than assertions. Take, for example, Daniel Deudney and G. John Ikenberry's recent essay in *Foreign Affairs*: they claim that "It is not inevitable that history will end with the triumph of liberalism, but it is inevitable that a decent world order will be liberal" and "the remedy for the problems of liberal democracy is more liberal democracy; liberalism contains the seeds of its own salvation".[17] Theirs is in an entirely circular argument whereby liberalism is responsible for all the advances but none of the setbacks, and a good, fair and decent order is by definition liberal. This position ignores not only that liberalism itself has a long history of illiberal ideas, including freedom without social solidarity (e.g. John Locke, Immanuel Kant, John Rawls), the primacy of the individual secured by the collective power of the state over civic associations (e.g. Thomas Hobbes, Jean-Jacques Rousseau, Friedrich von Hayek), or faith in a better future based on a secular metaphysics of progress (e.g. Auguste Comte, J.S. Mill, Steven Pinker). It also fails to recognise that liberalism has often been intolerant by ironing out plurality and closing down debate about the foundations of both domestic politics and international relations. These strands of intolerant liberalism bring about forms of liberal democracy that are neither liberal nor democratic – not just former transition countries but also the older democracies of the West. Illiberal liberalism has also created an international order that is in reality a Western-dominated disorder, as the remainder of this chapter suggests.

Sphere of influence or imperialism?

One principal problem with the defence of the liberal international order is a reliance on three core claims that are more wrong than right. First, that this order is the main reason for peace and prosperity since 1945. Second, that the key motivation of US foreign policy has been to create and uphold this order. Third, that Donald Trump and his support for fellow strongmen is the primary threat to the liberal order of peace and prosperity. But Graham Allison, in the same recent number of *Foreign Affairs*, rebuts the case by the advocates of liberal internationalism such as G. John Ikenberry:

> The "long peace" was the not the result of a liberal order but the by-product of the dangerous balance of power between the Soviet Union and the US during the four and a half decades of the Cold War and then of a brief period of US dominance. US engagement in the world has been driven not by the desire to advance liberalism abroad or to build an international order but by the need to do what was necessary to preserve liberal democracy at home. And although Trump is undermining key elements of the current order, he is far from the biggest threat to global stability.[18]

The other principal problem with the arguments in favour of the liberal world order is that they rest on a fundamental misconception of the nature of this order. Far from being a rules-based order (which is an oxymoron), the liberal international order is based on a sphere of influence in the sense of a conception of international order and an idea of due (or undue) influence on its constituent parts.[19] In other words, this sphere concerns questions of national sovereignty and foreign intervention, as it involves the possibility of interfering in the sovereign affairs of independent countries to preserve order and defend certain values that are liberal – including freedom, human rights, democracy and global free trade. Thus, the liberal international order is compatible with a specific sphere of influence that differs from other spheres of influence insofar as it rests on the principles of economic and political liberalism that are promoted by "great powers" beyond their borders, notably the US, the UK, continental European countries and Western allies elsewhere.[20]

Such a system is not the same as Bull's account of international society. The international society he conceptualised is less a society than an impersonal mechanism, which rests on the myth of sovereign equality. Ole Wæver puts this well:

> Bull, and a lot of Bullians, create a picture of the international *system* as a kind of "law of nature", a mechanical, timeless world of ultrarealism where international *society* then enters as the norms and rules; it is a picture closer to American neoliberalism with its interest in cooperation, regimes and institutions.[21]

Thus, US liberalism has championed an artificial state system based on American norms and rules, not a society composed of genuinely common values as well as shared interests and institutions. In fact, the origins of the liberal sphere of influence are traceable to the 1823 Monroe Doctrine and the 14-point plan by the US President Woodrow Wilson in 1919. Common to both is an opposition to colonialism and an emphasis on national self-determination, but also an accentuation on the pre-eminence of the US – starting with the US domination over its Central and Latin American "backyard" and progressively extending to the rest of the world.

While the imperial powers of France and Britain were greatly weakened by four years of unprecedented bloodshed and destruction, the other old empires of Tsarist Russia, Austro-Hungary, the Ottomans and Germany collapsed altogether. Newly independent countries across Central and Eastern Europe as well as the Balkans and the Middle East retained ties to Paris and London but found a new champion in the United States of America, which became the leading economic and geopolitical power. Paradoxically, the liberal order – which had begun as an anti-colonial project in 1776 and as a republican alternative to imperial monarchy (especially after 1789 and 1848) – morphed into a novel kind of imperialism led by the US. On his visit to London on Christmas Day 1918, Wilson declared in front of the assembled court of St James that the old order embodied by Britain was over and that the US represented a new dawn that would make the world "safe for democracy". In the process, the US elevated the Westphalian principle of national self-determination into the overriding criterion of the international system and, as the historian David Reynolds argues,

> the prime test of state legitimacy, rather than dynastic inheritance or imperial rule. Here indeed was a "seismic shift" in European history. Yet the principle of nationalism was an artificial construct, almost an anthropomorphic fantasy. Consider some of its cognate terms – national *consciousness*, national *will*, *self*-determination: in each case the nation is treated as analogous to an individual human being. [...] In short, [the aim of the US is] to recast the world in America's self-image.[22]

In other words, the Wilsonian account of international politics views national states as liberal egos writ large. This conception rests on liberal norms of individualism and voluntarist power that are deeply rooted in American political life and have been exported by successive US administrations that promote national ends by imperial means.[23] In this sense, Trump's motto to "make America great again" is in line with the implicit norms of US politics and not a fundamental departure from the quest for liberal hegemony, which locks the US and its allies in a "hell of good intentions" and "forever wars" that undermine Western democracies at home and their moral standing abroad.[24]

The origins of this quest go back not only to Wilson but also to the 1941 Atlantic Charter signed by US President Franklin D. Roosevelt and the British Prime Minister Winston Churchill, which added free trade to national self-determination as a foundational value. It represented a moment when, in the words of the historian David Ellwood, Roosevelt became personally convinced of the "universal significance of the American historical experience".[25] Thus, a specific idea of universalism underpins the institutions of the liberal world order with the US and its own sphere of influence at the core.

From Wilson via Roosevelt, Nixon and Reagan to the neo-conservative vision for a New American Century, the US gradually replaced the balance of power and national interests (the settlement established by the 1815 Congress of Vienna and only slightly qualified by the League of Nations) with a hegemony of fantasised universal values and global interests – a conception according to which American values and interests are synonymous with those of the rest of the world. Curiously, the US has always denied that it is in the business of building an empire. Instead, its leaders have argued that independent America came into existence precisely to throw off the shackles of British colonial rule and to fight imperialism everywhere. As the former US Defence Secretary Donald Rumsfeld famously said in an interview with Al-Jazeera, "We don't seek empires. We're not imperialistic. We never have been".[26] However, Karl Rove – a long-standing adviser of President George W. Bush – was rather more honest when he declared in the aftermath of the Iraq invasion that "We're an empire now, and when we act, we create our own reality".[27] Whether apocryphal or not, this statement encapsulates the peculiar liberal fusion of realism with idealism and the refashioning of the world in the image of liberalism.

The historian Niall Ferguson rightly remarked that "the United States is the empire that dares not speak its name. It is an empire in denial, and US denial of this poses a real danger to the world. An empire that doesn't recognise its own power is a dangerous one".[28] This is manifest in the protracted crisis of the liberal values-based foreign policy that was so dominant under Bill Clinton and Tony Blair's "humanitarian" interventionism and the neoconservative crusade in Afghanistan and Iraq.[29] At the same time, the US and its allies worldwide remain the single most powerful global force. With around 900 military bases in as many as three-quarters of the world's countries and 30 per cent of total global wealth, US power continues to exceed that of the British Empire at any point in history. If the liberal world order underwritten by American liberalism faces its greatest challenge to date, it is because this order tends towards hubris and is thus by nature unstable.

Liberal hubris

The key to understanding why liberalism faces the greatest threat to its domination since the rise of totalitarianism in the 1930s is the nature of the current crisis – liberal overreaching and the inherent contradictions of liberalism's tendency towards empire. Up to a point, the defenders of the liberal world order recognise the tension between the US role in the international system as *Liberal Leviathan* (Ikenberry) that upholds the rules-based structure and provides public goods, on the one hand, and the forces of reactionary nationalism in the US that undermines the liberal order and threatens to consume the global public goods, on the other hand.

However, one can go further than that to suggest that liberalism is so hubristic that it ends up cutting off the branch on which it sits. First there was liberal hubris after the end of the Cold War. Francis Fukuyama's "end of history" thesis captured the conceit that Western liberal market democracy is the final form of government to which all parts of the world will ultimately converge. As Ivan Krastev puts it, "The Western model was the only (i)deal in town".[30] For the advocates of the liberal order, the post-1989 world was one in which borders would formally endure even while losing much of their real relevance. Robert Reich, Clinton's Secretary of Labor, described the new model of political economy in the following terms: "There will be no *national* products or technologies, no national corporations, no national industries. There will no longer be national economies. At least as we have come to understand that concept".[31] So when the Soviet bloc imploded, and free-market capitalism replaced state communism, progressives and neo-conservatives talked of a liberal world order and a new American century.

Yet the end of communism inaugurated in reality "the new world disorder", as Stanley Hoffmann and Ken Jowitt argued in different ways.[32] The events of 1989 and 1991 were not primarily an hour of triumphal victory of one ideology and system over its rival but rather an epoch of crisis and disruption as a result of the implosion of the Soviet system. Contrary to the borderless utopia of liberal progressivism, critical voices like Hoffmann and Jowitt anticipated the redrawing of borders, the reshaping of national identities, an escalation of previously frozen conflicts and paralysing uncertainty rather than post-ideological clarity. What liberalism's short-lived hegemony concealed from view was a resurgence of old ethno-national and religious identities and the rise to power of alternative worldviews with a claim to universal validity, notably capitalism (compatible as much with liberal democracy as with illiberal authoritarianism) and Islamism.[33] With the weakening of national states by globalisation,[34] movements of contestation and rage sprung up across the world – from the new social movements and Al-Qaeda in the late 1990s via Occupy Wall Street after 2007–2008 to the Arab Spring and ISIS since 2010.

Faced with threats to democracy from Islamism, the war on terror and the destructive power of finance in the post-Cold War era, liberals failed to heed not just Hoffmann's and Jowitt's scepticism but also the prescient warning by George Kennan in 1957 when he said the following in his BBC Reith Lectures:

There is, let me assure you, nothing in nature more egocentric than the embattled democracy. It soon becomes the victim of its own war propaganda. It then tends to attach to its own cause an absolute value which distorts everything else. *Its* enemy becomes the embodiment of all evil. *Its* own side, on the other hand, is the center of all virtue. The contest comes to be viewed as having a final, apocalyptic quality. If *we* lose, all is lost; life will no longer be worth living; there will be nothing to be salvaged. If we win, then everything will be possible; all our problems will become soluble; the one great source of evil – *our* enemy – will have been crushed; the forces of good will then sweep forward unimpeded; all worthy aspirations will be satisfied.[35]

It is perhaps unsurprising that the advocates of the liberal world order have therefore been in denial about their own role in the crisis of the international system which has been in place since 1945. What started off as a rules-based system organised around cooperation between sovereign states and the embedding of markets in institutions morphed after 1989 into a US-led world order, which promotes free-market globalisation, mass migration and military intervention in the name of supposedly universal, but in reality, Western, narrowly liberal values.

At every point, liberals gave in to the siren calls of hubris. After 9/11, the wars in Afghanistan, Iraq, Libya and Syria exacerbated the threat from Islamic fundamentalists while shredding the West's moral standing. The financial crash of 2008 destroyed the US-created "Washington consensus" of free-market fundamentalism, yet the liberal elites rewarded greed and failure by bailing out banks while workers lost their jobs and communities struggled with debt. 2016 was the year when the ghosts of liberal capitalism came back to haunt the establishment. For the first time since the Second World War, Brexit and Trump have given the economic losers a political victory over the economic winners and ejected liberals from power. Together, Brexit and Trump have buried once and for all the idea that the liberal model of globalisation ushered in the "end of history" – the conceit that the Western brand of market capitalism is the only valid model because it produces more benefits than losses or, in utilitarian terms, the "greatest happiness of the greatest number".

Gone with it is the post-1945 promise of progress for every generation. According to a recent study by the Pew Research Center, the American middle class, once the largest class and the very meaning of the "American Dream", is the majority no longer. In the UK, the government's social mobility commission found in its annual "state of the nation" reports in 2016 and 2017 that the Thatcher generation growing up during the 1980s and the millennials are the first cohort since 1945 to start their career on lower incomes than their parents.

In short, Brexit and Trump are insurgencies against this dogmatic liberalism and its advocates – the progressive modernisers on the left and the right who brought us a creed of low wages, deindustrialisation, job-exporting trade deals, the deregulation of global finance and endless war.

Contemporary liberalism is even more corrosive than that. Liberal economics reinforced social liberalism with its celebration of diversity and emancipation through ever-greater freedom of choice. Never did the political mainstream consider how the promotion of minority interests might affect the rest of the economy, society or the globe at large. Instead, liberals privileged individual happiness over social solidarity while entrenching power and wealth for the fortunate few.[36] For all the important advancement in terms of equality and non-discrimination, progressive liberalism alienated more socially conservative voters who are predominantly indigenous but also include many ethnic minorities. Far from being an endangered species, these voters represent a majority as most people choose a fairly traditional family structure, value their settled ways of life and are generally sceptical about the pace of change.

By tearing down trade barriers and borders, left- and right-wing progressives built a world of mobility and permanent revolution that overwhelmingly enriched a new establishment dominated by a certain professional class.[37] This class is composed of a "tech oligarchy" of hedge-fund managers, techno-scientific experts and self-made billionaires who pose simultaneously as free-market champions and liberal humanitarians, driven as they are in equal measure by supposedly "enlightened" self-interest and a sanctimonious pretence of moral superiority.[38] Treating with contempt both the traditional base of the left and the natural constituency of the right, the liberal modernisers have patronised or simply ignored those who neither supported this version of liberal politics nor benefitted from its effects – those for whom free trade, open borders and cosmopolitan multiculturalism have meant greater economic hardship and unnerving cultural comprises.

Liberal ideas have not suddenly gone from triumphalist to extinct, and many liberal institutions will endure. But liberalism, including liberal internationalism, faces an existential crisis because as a philosophy and a way of doing international politics it turns out to be contradictory and self-defeating. Its individualism undermines the dignity of the person and its fusion of state with market power erodes freedom. As a result, liberalism is permanently caught in a contradiction between release and control, which hollows out the social bonds and civic ties on which democracy and a market economy depend. Over time, this contradiction engenders not just periodic crises in a seemingly cyclical pattern of history but also a crisis of first principles and final ends because liberalism goes against the grain of humanity and erodes the cultural foundations on which it rests. For liberals assume that human beings are selfish, greedy, distrustful of others and prone to violence – either by nature (Hobbes and Locke) or through life in society (Rousseau and Kant) – unless the artifice of state sovereignty, transnational markets and international cooperation constrains them.[39]

Linking together the different strands of the liberal tradition is the premise that individual rights and freedoms are more fundamental than mutual obligations or the common good. Liberals look to the central state together with the free market as the ultimate arbiters to protect individuals from one another. But this conceals from view the collusion of state and market against society and the intermediary institutions that compose it. Those institutions include professional guilds, trade unions, religious communities, volunteer organisations, civic networks and other forms of human association that are self-governing rather than privatised or nationalised. It is precisely the impersonal forces of market-states that those left behind by cosmopolitan globalisation are now rejecting.

How liberalism undermines Western civilisation

One can go even further to argue the West's hegemonic power is weakening precisely because its underlying liberalism has progressively undermined the very foundations of Western civilisation. Part of the liberal appeal was the promise of progress, but liberalism unleashed the forces of science and technology while divorcing modernisation from the pursuit of substantive shared ends. In this manner, liberal ideology became increasingly associated with subjugating both nature and society to individual volition and with releasing the collective "will to power". A few prophetic voices warned against such voluntarism and the subversion of virtues. Fyodor Dostoevsky in *The Devils* and Joseph Conrad in *The Secret Agent* anatomised the secular extremists who embraced nineteenth-century positivism and nihilism in pursuit of a revolutionary vanguard whose origins go back to the Jacobins, the first exemplary inflictors of modern "terror".[40] And they also saw that this apparently shocking minority is, in reality, symptomatic of a wider terroristic tendency. Dostoevsky's dictum that "without God, everything is permitted" rightly indicated that ethics would be increasingly subordinated to politics, and politics to the iron law of power – the sheer strength of individual self-assertion and collective mobilisation, exemplified by mass conscription and total war since the French Revolution, Bonaparte and Bismarck.[41] While liberalism seeks to temper the worst excesses of human nature and realism by imposing constitutional-legal constraints,

As the historian Christopher Dawson argued in 1942, it is surely no coincidence that in the run-up to the two world wars, Western civilisation "suffered such a total subversion of its own standards and values while its material power and wealth remained almost intact, and in many respects greater than ever".[42] Unlike ancient despotism that had deployed brutal physical coercion, the positivist and nihilist ideas that many nineteenth-century liberals celebrated used the resources of modern psychology and mass propaganda to enlist both body and soul. The new liberal creed of progress, equality and emancipation displaced Greco-Roman and Christian values of the dignity of the person and the freedom of association around shared substantive objectives, which – as Nietzsche himself remarked – "prevented man from despising himself as man, from turning against life, and from being driven to despair by knowledge".[43] Thus the ambivalence of liberalism lies in the tendency to release human energy and foster individual freedoms while at the same time failing to guide the forces it unleashes on an international as well as national scale.

Instead of the culturally amalgamated society of nations, which once composed the West, liberalism has supported an artificial state system wherein membership is defined exclusively in terms of central sovereign power without any reference to the national character of the societies in question. When, in 1918, Woodrow Wilson elevated the "self-determination of people" into an absolute principle (which still governs the inter-state system to this day), he did not so much defend popular sovereignty or the consent of the governed for all the nations; rather, he encouraged the process of empire-breaking and state-building that inaugurated liberal hegemony and led to new wars. Wilson also called for the creation of an international organisation – the League of Nations – based on the equal rights of each participant member. This, as Dawson noticed, amounted to the recognition of every *de facto* state as a *de iure* nation (or identifiable "people") and treated a multiplicity of incommensurable political systems all alike – as though they were individuals writ large who are endowed with equal rights and a common nature.

Over time, according to Dawson, the liberal destruction of the medieval society of nations in favour of an inter-state system left peoples and societies exposed to two competing, yet mutually empowering, forces:

> The modern world is being driven along at the same time in two opposite directions. On the one hand the nations are being brought into closer contact by the advance of scientific and technical achievement; the limits of space and time that held them asunder are being contracted or abolished, and the world has become physically one as never before. On the other hand, the nations are being separated from one another by a process of intensive organization which weakens the spiritual links that bound men together irrespective of political frontiers and concentrates the whole energy of society on the attainment of a collective purpose, so as inevitably to cause a collision with the collective will of other societies. … What makes the danger of war so great today is … the death-grapple of huge impersonal mass Powers [sic] which have ground out the whole life of the whole population in the wheels of their social mechanism.[44]

The simultaneous interdependence of national societies and the sundering of social, cultural and religious ties that bind people together within and across state borders suggest that liberal hegemony faces an existential crisis, as I indicated earlier. This is in contrast to a mere systemic crisis, which would be to do with external threats to the inter-state system (say from a rogue, revisionist state), or the internal failure to secure a proper balance of power between sovereign states with rival interests. For, instead, it is the founding liberal assumptions for international order that are eventually being shaken through their own operation. Alongside the revival of political Islam, this is the real reason for the growing anarchy in international affairs.

This profound cultural malaise has affected the West's ability to shape the contemporary world. US military might and European economic expansion can scarcely hide the absence of any substantive accord among Western powers. As the US and European response to the "Arab Spring", events in Ukraine and now ISIS shows, there is a strategic void. The twilight of the West in the sense of the unquestioned hegemony of the Atlantic community could now be upon us.[45] Compared with the era since the discovery of the New World or even the recent Cold War past, the West today looks bereft of ideas, deeply divided and incapable of acting as a force for good amid ever-greater global interdependence and volatility, Western countries now oscillate between market anarchy and coercive state control. They eschew global leadership and lasting involvement abroad in favour of managing risks from afar.[46] Across the West, there is a growing populist backlash against the dominant forms of globalisation and there are calls to retreat to narrow national self-interest led by insurgent parties – above all, the forces behind Brexit and Trump. The liberal elites fail to understand that these forces are not simply given but in large part a consequence, not the cause, of the failure of liberalism.

Notes

1 John Gerald Ruggie, 'International Regimes, Transactions, and Change: Embedded Liberalism in the Postwar Economic Order', *International Organization*, Vol. 36, no. 2 (Spring 1982), pp. 379–415; *idem.*, 'Taking Embedded Liberalism Global: The Corporate Connection', in David Held and Mathias Koenig-Archibugi (eds.), *Taming Globalization: Frontiers of Governance* (Cambridge: Polity Press, 2003), pp. 93–129.
2 Hedley Bull, *The Anarchical Society: A Study of Order in World Politics* (London: Macmillan, 1996).
3 Joseph S. Nye, Jr, 'Will the Liberal Order Survive?', *Foreign Affairs*, Vol. 96, no. 1 (Jan.–Feb. 2017), pp. 10–16.
4 Francis Fukuyama, 'The End of History?', *The National Interest*, Vol. 16 (Summer 1989), pp. 3–18, expanded as *The End of History and the Last Man* (New York: The Free Press, 1992).
5 Robin Niblett, 'Liberalism in Retreat: The Demise of a Dream', *Foreign Affairs*, Vol. 96, no. 1 (Jan.–Feb. 2017), pp. 17–24.
6 Barry Eichengreen, *Exorbitant Privilege: The Rise and Fall of the Dollar and the Future of the International Monetary System* (New York: Oxford University Press, 2010).

7 See the trilogy by Joseph S. Nye, Jr, *Bound to Lead: The Changing Nature of American Power* (New York: Basic Books, 1990); *Soft Power: The Means to Success in World Politics* (New York: Public Affairs, 2004); *The Future of Power* (New York: Public Affairs, 2011).

8 Adrian Pabst, *The Demons of Liberal Democracy* (Cambridge: Polity Press, 2019).

9 See again Nye, 'Will the Liberal Order Survive?' and Niblett, 'Liberalism in Retreat: The Demise of a Dream'.

10 G. John Ikenberry, *Liberal Leviathan: The Origins, Crisis and Transformation of the American World Order* (Princeton, NJ: Princeton University Press, 2011).

11 G. John Ikenberry, 'The Liberal International Order and Its Discontents', *Millennium: Journal of International Studies*, Vol. 38, No. 3 (2010), pp. 509–521, quote at p. 514.

12 G. John Ikenberry, 'Liberal Internationalism 3.0: America and the Dilemmas of Liberal World Order', *Perspectives on Politics*, Vol. 7, no 1 (2009), pp. 71–87.

13 Michael Cox, 'Power and the Liberal Order', in *After Liberalism? The Future of Liberalism in International Relations*, ed. Rebekka Friedman, Kevork Oskanian and Ramon Pacheco Pardo (London: Palgrave-Macmillan, 2013), pp. 103–116.

14 Walter Russell Mead, 'The Jacksonian Revolt: American Populism and the Liberal Order', *Foreign Affairs* Vol. 96, no. (April 2017), pp. 2–7.

15 President Xi Jinping, Address to the World Economic Forum in Davos, 17 January 2017, available online at www.weforum.org/agenda/2017/01/full-text-of-xi-jinping-keynote-at-the-world-economic-forum

16 President Donald J. Trump, The Inaugural Address, 20 January 2017, available online at www.whitehouse.gov/inaugural-address

17 Daniel Deudney and G. John Ikenberry, 'Liberal World: The Resilient Order', *Foreign Affairs*, Vol. 97, no. 4 (July/August 2018), pp. 16–24, quotes at p. 16 and 18.

18 Graham Allison, 'The Myth of the Liberal Order: From Historical Accident to Conventional Wisdom', *Foreign Affairs*, Vol. 97, no. 4 (July/August 2018), pp. 124–133, quote at p. 125.

19 Susanna Hast, *Spheres of Influence in International Relations: History, Theory and Politics* (Aldershot: Ashgate, 2014).

20 John Mearsheimer, *The Tragedy of Great Power Politics* (New York: Norton, 2001).

21 Ole Wæver, 'Imperial Metaphors: Emerging European Analogies to Pre-Nation-State Imperial Systems', in O. Tunander, P. Baev and V.I. Einangel (eds.), *Geopolitics in Post-Wall Europe* (London: Sage Publications, 1997), pp. 59–93, quote at p. 62.

22 David Reynolds, *The Long Shadow: The Great War and the Twentieth Century* (London: Schuster & Schuster, 2013), pp. 15 and 37 (original italics).

23 Michael Northcott, *An Angel Directs the Storm: Apocalyptic Religion and American Empire* (London: I.B. Tauris, 2004); William Pfaff, *The Irony of Manifest Destiny: The Tragedy of American Foreign Policy* (New York: Walker and Company, 2010).

24 Stephen M. Walt, *The Hell of Good Intentions: America's Foreign Policy Elite and the Decline of U.S. Primacy* (New York: Farrar Straus and Giroux, 2018).

25 David W. Ellwood, *Rebuilding Europe: Western Europe, America and Post war Reconstruction* (London: Longman, 1992), p. 21.

26 Quoted in Noel Maurer, *The Empire Trap: The Rise and Fall of US Intervention to Protect American Property Overseas (1893–2013)* (Princeton, NJ: Princeton University Press, 2013).

27 Quoted in Ron Suskind, 'Faith, Certainty and the Presidency of George W. Bush', *New York Times* Magazine, 17 October 2004, available online at www.nytimes.com/2004/10/17/magazine/17BUSH.html?_r=3&ex=125566 5600&en=890a96189e162076&ei=5090&partner=rssuserland&

28 In remarks at the 2003 Hay Festival, quoted in *The Guardian* 2 June 2003, available online at www.theguardian.com/uk/2003/jun/02/highereducation.books; see also Niall Ferguson, *Colossus: The Rise and Fall of the American Empire* (London: Penguin, 2009).

29 Michael Ignatieff, *Empire Lite: National Building in Bosnia, Kosovo and Afghanistan* (New York: Vintage, 2003); for an alternative liberal view on humanitarian intervention, see David Rieff, *A Bed for the Night: Humanitarianism in Crisis* (New York: Schuster and Schuster, 2002) and *idem.*, 'R2P, R.I.P.', *The New York Times*, 7 November 2011.

30 Krastev, 'The Unraveling of the Post-1989 Order', p. 6.

31 Robert B. Reich, *The Work of Nations: Preparing Ourselves for 21st-century Capitalism* (New York: Vintage 1992), p. 3 (original italics).

32 Ken Jowitt, 'After Leninism: The New World Disorder', *Journal of Democracy* Vol. 2, no. 1 (Winter 1991), pp. 11–20, expanded as *The New World Disorder: The Leninist Extinction* (Berkeley, CA: University of California Press, 1992); Stanley Hoffmann, *World Disorders: Troubled Peace in the Post-Cold War Era* (New York: Rowman & Littlefield, 1998).

33 Mark Juergensmeyer, *The New Cold War? Religious Nationalism Confronts the Secular State* (Berkeley, CA: University of California Press, 1993); *Terror in the Mind of God: The Global Rise of Religious Violence* (Berkeley, CA: University of California Press, 2000).

34 Robert Cooper, *The Breaking of Nations: Order and Chaos in the Twenty-first Century*, 2nd ed. (London: Atlantic Books, 2007).

35 George F. Kennan, *Russia and the West Under Lenin and Stalin* (New York: Mentor Books, 1960), p. 11 (original italics).

36 David J. Rothkopf, *Superclass: The Global Power Elite and the World They Are Making* (London: Little, Brown & Company, 2008); Ferdinand Mount, *The New Few, Or a Very British Oligarchy* (London: Simon & Schuster, 2012); Chrystia Freeland, *Plutocrats: The Rise of the New Global Super-Rich and the Fall of Everyone Else* (London: Penguin, 2013).

37 Thomas Frank, *Listen, Liberal: Or, What Ever Happened to the Party of the People?* (London: Scribe, 2016); Joel Kotkin, *The New Class Conflict* (Candor, NY: Telos Publishing Press, 2014).

38 Thomas G. Weiss, *Humanitarian Business* (Cambridge: Polity Press, 2012).

39 For a longer exposition of this thesis, see John Milbank and Adrian Pabst, *The Politics of Virtue. Post-liberalism and the Human Future* (London: Rowman & Littlefield, 2016).

40 John Gray, *Al Qaeda and What It Means to Be Modern* (London: Faber and Faber, 2003).

41 David A. Bell, *The First Total War: Napoleon's Europe and the Birth of Warfare as We Know It* (New York: Mariner, 2008).

42 Christopher Dawson, *The Judgment of the Nations* (Washington: The Catholic University of America Press, 2011), p. 7.

43 Quoted in *ibid.*, p. 9.
44 *Ibid.*, p. 52.
45 Christopher Coker, *Twilight of the West* (London: Basic Books, 1997).
46 Ulrich Beck, *Risk Society: Towards a New Modernity*, tr. Mark Ritter (London: Sage, 2002); *World at Risk* (Cambridge: Polity Press, 2009); Christopher Coker, *War in an Age of Risk* (Cambridge: Polity Press, 2009).

2 Backlash

The global revolt against liberalism

The new disorder

The claim that the liberal world order has not fundamentally changed in recent years fails to recognise the nature and sheer scale of the current crisis. The post-1989 order is unravelling and liberal Europe is in retreat.[1] After the Brexit vote, a full or partial disintegration of the EU is more plausible than at any point since the signing of the Rome Treaties 60 years ago. Across the EU, member-states face either the prospect of break-up (the UK, Belgium, Spain) or anti-establishment insurgencies that threaten the existence of the Euro and the functioning of the Union. Neither national nor community institutions have prevented the rise of illiberal governments in member-states such as Hungary and Poland – including an assault on the freedom and independence of courts, NGOs and the media, combined with growing ideological polarisation and a political witch-hunt of the official opposition.

In what follows, I will return to the so-called populist reaction against liberalism. But for now, it makes sense to note that a slide into the extremism of the far left and the radical right is no longer unthinkable. After all, Trump has captured the GOP and his wider team have injected "alt-right" themes into the political mainstream. Meanwhile, Jeremy Corbyn and the militant movement Momentum have taken charge of the Labour Party and stand a realistic chance of forming the next UK government, which has already happened with Syriza in Greece. An increasingly authoritarian Turkey may see its status of EU accession country rescinded and could even face expulsion from NATO. While these scenarios seemed impossible just a few years ago, they are now merely improbable.

The election of Donald Trump is so far the single greatest blow against the liberal world order. His political outlook seems to combine certain nationalist-libertarian ideas with a preference for populist-authoritarian leadership at home and abroad. The red thread that runs through his rhetoric over the past 30 years is an anti-liberal assault on the implicit bipartisan consensus at the heart of American politics: free trade, immigration and the US promotion of Western forms of democracy and human rights. While the retreat from the Trans-Pacific Partnership (TPP) might extend an olive branch to Beijing, the threat of protectionism has not disappeared altogether and could yet trigger a trade war with China. His comments on the obsolete character of NATO also raise the prospect of weakening the transatlantic alliance in favour of bilateral relations based on transactional deals.

More generally, Trump's presidency could mark a rupture in the bipartisan support of US foreign policy for the past 70 years. Undermined by bad trade deals, short-changed by free-riding allies and dragged into endless military campaigns, Trump believes it is time for the US to refuse to expend more blood and treasure propping up an international system that he reckons will continue to weaken the US. Both on the campaign trail and in the first two years of his term in office, Trump has claimed that trade deals such as NAFTA and the now-cancelled TPP destroy American jobs and move employment to lower-wage countries that manipulate their currency. While the US spends billions of dollars of taxes paid by ordinary Americans in order to finance its worldwide security umbrella, free riders in Europe and Asia get rich by shirking their responsibilities for burden-sharing. The inability of other powers to sort out instability in their own backyards forces the US to step in and intervene militarily – leaving behind a mountain of debt (a staggering US $1.3 trillion in the case of Afghanistan alone) and a tainted reputation. Seen in this light, it is no surprise that Trump and his team reject the raw deal they think the US gets and that they want to create a new international order – more of a balance-of-powers order based on national interest rather than a liberal order based on supposedly universal values.

None of this is particularly new in US politics. In 1992, Pat Buchanan ran for the Republican nomination promising a mix of mercantilism and greater geopolitical restraint. Half a century earlier, Senator Robert Taft – who failed to become the Republican nominee in 1940, 1948 and 1952 – advocated American isolationism before the Second World War and thereafter opposed President Truman's policy to expand trade. His anti-communism did not stop him from opposing the strategy of containment and the creation of NATO because it would over-commit the US. Trump's penchant for President Putin and other strongmen is also, as Thomas Wright has argued, "reminiscent of Charles Lindbergh, once an American hero, who led the isolationist America First movement. In some areas, Trump's views go back even further, to 19th-century high-tariff protectionism and every-country-for-itself mercantilism".[2]

What drives the Trump administration is anger about the bad deal the country supposedly gets from the liberal international order upheld by US hegemony since 1945 and especially after 1989. The new president is opposed to the military alliances that are subsidised by American taxpayers, the trade arrangements that export jobs and import immigrants, as well as the promotion of liberal democracy that antagonises fellow "great powers" like Russia while harming the national self-interest of the US. Anti-liberalism on economic, social, and geopolitical issues seems to be the common ground with Vladimir Putin. Both believe that their countries have not benefitted from the liberal model of globalisation, which is why Trump wants to roll back free trade and immigration while Putin is trying to opt out in favour of parallel structures – starting with greater protection from global forces for the national economies of neighbouring countries that join the Eurasian Economic Union.[3] The leaders of Russia and the US are also united in rejecting the "open-border progressivism" of liberal governments across the West and want to put national greatness ahead of minority demands.

Many politicians and pundits will dismiss it as an alliance of reactionaries (*à la* Lindbergh and Hitler) or a new Populist International that also includes Britain's UKIP and France's Marine Le Pen.[4] The aim is seemingly to get allies of the US in Asia and Europe to pay their fair share for the US security umbrella and to tone down the level of vitriol in order to avert an escalation with Moscow that might end in war – though the rivalry in Syria could yet get out of hand. Judging by Trump's actions in the first two years after inauguration, his victory will likely mark the continued decline of the post-1945 liberal order that has been in retreat since 9/11 and the 2008 financial crash. What might replace it and what happens next is anyone's guess. Will it be more global anarchy and a slide into direct confrontation between the US and China? Or else some new order based on non-liberal institutions and rules, perhaps akin to a nineteenth-century type "great power" concert in a new guise with an implicit recognition of spheres of influence? Either way, the tectonic plates have already shifted and the unfolding earthquake is only just beginning to engulf the West and the rest.

Liberal and illiberal populism

Across the world there are protest movements and insurgent parties that are mobilising against the liberalism that underpins the international order. Examples include the *Front National* and *La France Insoumise* in France; the Scottish National Party and the UK Independence Party in Britain; the *Alternative für Deutschland* and Pegida in Germany; Golden Dawn and Syriza in Greece; the Danish People's Party; the Sweden Democrat;

The Party for Freedom in the Netherlands; the Freedom Party in Austria; the True Finns; the Tea Party in the US and now the "alt right" around Trump. Whatever their important ideological differences, the new populists are all staunchly anti-establishment and purport to speak for the voiceless, the angry and the disaffected – an appeal to both working- and middle-class people who feel alienated from the mainstream parties, have lost out from globalisation and do not want to lose their national identity.

The mainstream parties are struggling and many are losing power. In Spain, there are now four – not just two – parties vying for power, and the same is true for Germany (the centre-right CDU/CSU, the right-wing AfD, the SPD and the far-left Die Linke). In Greece, the socialist party PASOK has gone from winning 44 per cent of the vote in 2009 to 4 per cent in 2015. In the US, the anti-establishment insurgency of Bernie Sanders nearly beat Hillary Clinton to the nomination, while Donald Trump eliminated 15 rivals among the Republicans and won the presidential election that was Clinton's to lose. Italy's centre-left and centre-right lost the March 2018 elections to the populists of Lega and the Five Star Movement, whose coalition combines a far-right politics on immigration and identity with far-left politics on economic intervention and welfare for the indigenous population. As Jamie Bartlett has argued, the leader of the Five Star Movement Beppe Grillo embodies the dangers of digital populism:

> Like all populists he pits the good, honest, ordinary citizen against the out-of-touch professional political class. He vows to represent the pure people, the 'we', against the morally corrupt elite, the "them". An authentic and honest voice in a nihilistic political world of spin and self-interest. This is a dangerous narrative that can lead to some dark corners – anything can be justified in the name of the people.[5]

Just as establishment liberalism can take an intolerant turn, so too the anti-elite insurgency embraces the anti-liberal ideas of general will from Rousseau via Comte and Mill to Marx.

Nor is this shift from mainstream to insurgent parties or candidates limited to North America and Western Europe. In Latin America, the democratic socialists who have been in power for the past 20 or so are losing ground: in Argentina, they have already been evicted from power, while they are struggling in Venezuela and Brazil. Similarly, in Eastern Europe, Ukraine and Turkey outsiders are fighting the establishment, often polarising and radicalising national politics – such as Jobbik in Hungary or Right Sector in Ukraine.

In response, mainstream parties seek to occupy and expand the middle ground. They desperately try to tack both left and right in order to head off the far-left or far-right opposition – talking tough on immigration (Emmanuel Macron) and promising more state intervention in the market (Theresa May). However, as the establishment converged for decades towards a centrist liberal position, the extremes have been growing in strength. The far-left Syriza party has won twice in Greece and is governing in coalition with a nationalist-conservative party. Brexit and Trump might just be the beginning, with the radical right in the ascendancy in France and Italy. And that is not to mention the power of strongmen in countries as diverse as Russia, China, the Philippines, India or Japan. Linking together the popular support for Presidents Putin, Xi and Duterte, as well as Prime Ministers Modi and Abe, is that they oppose a liberal elite (domestic or international or both at once) and purport to stand up for ordinary citizens who feel that liberal globalisation is synonymous with a system rigged in favour of insiders.

A new narrative is taking hold among liberal elites that their political rivals are authoritarian populists who want to bring down the liberal world order and banish its defenders. But the problem with notions such as "authoritarianism" or "populism" is that they can apply to establishment liberals just as much as to insurgents on the revolutionary left or the far right. Authoritarian methods have been used by governing parties across the political spectrum to override the official opposition in parliament and quash extra-parliamentary resistance. Populist means, including vote-winning manipulations of the electorate, have never been the monopoly of insurgents who are just as elite as the establishment.

Left- and right-wing liberals who complain about authoritarian populists forget their own role in the rise of the latest political insurgency. First, they fused politics with the media, circumventing the constraints of parliamentary democracy in favour of a direct line with the people mediated mostly by Murdoch and the *Mail*. Anthony Barnett is right to describe this system of government as a form of manipulative corporate populism.[6] It represents a political tactic exemplified by Bill Clinton's and New Labour's culture of spin and George Osborne's Project Fear. Both gained and retained office for some time but ended up being rejected by the people.

Now the label "populist" is used for political movements with popular backing for ideas of which liberal elites disapprove. By pursuing an ultra-liberal project to which "there is no alternative", the Western political class has sown the seeds of its own downfall. The electoral success of Justin Trudeau, Emmanuel Macron and Angela Merkel shows how liberal leaders can defeat their anti-liberal foes. But the rising tide of discontent suggests that the liberal centre ground is hollow. Liberal democracy is straining under the weight of its own inner contradiction between market anarchy and state control.

Since Antiquity, philosophers have cautioned against the slide of democracy into oligarchy, demagogy and tyranny. Today, this warning applies to liberalism and the dangers it poses to democratic rule. Liberalism, far from defending open markets, maintains old monopolies and creates new cartels. Ten years after the financial crisis, banking conglomerates are still "too big to fail" and senior bankers who have broken the law "too big to jail". In 2017, two-thirds of the 900 sectors of Western economies exhibit a greater concentration of ownership and control than in 1997. This is distorting prices, consumer choice and the quality products and services from banking via water to food. Amazon, Apple, Facebook and Google are modern-day plutocracies with dominant market positions. They take over their online competitors and the traditional retail world. By managing access to information and knowledge, these tech giants exercise control over public debate in ways that threaten not just open markets but also free speech. Plutocratic power undermines economic competition and democracy, and it tends to engender a Caesarian revolt, as with Trump's victory.

This drift towards oligarchy also reveals how liberalism is a catalyst for demagogy. Liberal thought rests on the assumption that only liberalism can free us from the tyranny of the Good – the imposition of a single conception of goodness, truth and beauty. The liberal tradition with its securing of individual rights has certainly provided more opportunities and greater freedom from oppression, but the price liberal societies pay is replacing substantive notions of the good with empty free choice. Liberty is now the absence of constraints on individual desire except for the law and private conscience. Liberal freedom to choose is manipulative because the conditions under which choice is exercised are not up for debate and those who do not succeed on liberalism's terms only have themselves to blame.

The liberal indifference to substantive values also involves a tendency to exploit fear and manipulate opinion. Liberalism claims to offer security by guarding us against alien elements – the terrorist, the bigot, the racist, the welfare-scrounger and those deemed deficient in "entrepreneurship". For liberals, human beings are rational, self-owning individuals who owe nothing to society. The name for this liberal philosophy, first developed by Hobbes and Locke in the seventeenth century, is possessive individualism and existing liberalism promotes both rampant egotism and a sense that only property has value.[7]

Liberalism also separates fact from value and privileges enlightened elites over the common sense of the people, as George Orwell first diagnosed. That is why contemporary liberal democracy is caught between the factual truth of technocrats and the emotive "post-truth" of so-called populists. For liberals, everything can be debated publicly – including the personal, private sphere – except the dangers of liberalism. The liberal practice of oligarchy and demagogy ends up undermining the principles of liberality on which liberalism rests, including free inquiry, free speech and tolerance. Liberal politics thereby produces the threats that it supposedly protects us from – ideological tyranny and the closing-down of argument. University "safe spaces" and echo chambers on social media leave people unprepared to deal with views other than their own. The result is a political culture that is increasingly narcissistic and unable to build broad alliances, as exemplified by Hillary Clinton's minority politics.

Paradoxically, liberalism brings about the kind of intolerant illiberalism that it ascribes to all non-liberal positions. What liberals demonise as populism is in large part a backlash against liberalism without democracy by movements that seek to institute a democracy without liberalism. Anti-establishment insurgents frequently try to override constitutional limits on power in ways that change the character and substance of the rule of law while also repudiating the policies of mass immigration, worldwide free trade and democracy promotion on which the liberal world order rests. But illiberal populism is to some extent a corrective of liberal corporate populism: "in a world that is dominated by democracy and liberalism, populism has essentially become an illiberal democratic response to undemocratic liberalism. Populists ask uncomfortable questions about undemocratic aspects of liberal institutions and policies".[8] These questions include globalisation, immigration and national identity, which have been excluded from the political agenda and public debate. Without a genuine debate about such fundamental questions, the liberal world order will continue to lack legitimacy in the West and beyond.

The end of economic progress

A significant element of the appeal of anti-establishment insurgencies, which oppose the liberal world order, is that mainstream parties have failed to fulfil their promise about prosperity. Across advanced economies, hard-working families are experiencing more and more economic uncertainty and cultural insecurity.[9] Their incomes are declining, their jobs are disappearing and their identity is under threat – from global capitalism (and its aggressive liberal culture), from mass immigration and from forces such as Islamic extremism and terrorism. All this is fuelling a popular revolt against the establishment that is wedded to the international system of the *status quo*.

The standard analysis in terms of the political left or the political right does not explain this situation very convincingly. Nor do standard left-wing or right-wing responses solve the profound structural problems precisely because they are part of the same liberal logic – more state or more market. Why have average working people in advanced economies such as the US or the UK lost out? Why are their incomes declining and their jobs becoming more precarious? Both the left and the right claim that this is the price we must pay for the advantages of globalisation and technological change. In other words, the benefits of progress are bigger than the costs. For example, industrial and manufacturing production – steel, chemicals, cars and so on – can now be done more cheaply either by lower-paid workers abroad (or cheap immigrants) or by computer-driven machines – including robots, digitised production, artificial intelligence and automation.[10]

In response to this supposed necessity of globalisation and technological change, the political left wants an interventionist state that raises taxes on the rich and the tech companies, and redistributes the revenue to the poor while also investing in more university education. Meanwhile, the political right rejects all this because it believes that wealth will trickle down: if government is limited, public spending is lower and taxes and regulation are minimal, the economy will boom and everyone will be better off. The problem is that both are wrong in their analysis and in their policy solutions. Taxation and regulation have not solved inequality, as Thomas Piketty has demonstrated in his book *Capital in the Twenty-First Century*.[11] Nor does the economy generate enough jobs that pay people enough to feed themselves and their families. Just look at the explosion in the number of people who depend on food stamps in the US or on food banks in the UK – working families, not just the unemployed or homeless.

The fundamental reason, as the US economist and former labour secretary Robert Reich has argued, is "the increasing concentration of political power in a corporate and financial elite that has been able to influence the rules by which the economy runs".[12] We have a rampant form of corporate finance capitalism that works for the top 20 per cent, but not for the remaining 80 per cent.[13] It pays exorbitant salaries to the top managements and huge bonuses, even when their businesses are not growing or going bust – as big banks like Lehman Brothers or multinational corporations such as Enron or WorldCom. This system is economically dysfunctional and ethically bankrupt, leading to a situation where – to quote Reich again – "the fracture in politics will move from left to right to the anti-establishment versus establishment".[14]

Examples what this means in reality abound. First of all, the ratio of highest to lowest incomes in companies has grown exponentially, from 30:1 or 40:1 to 300:1 or even 450:1. Second, the top 1 per cent in the US own about 30 per cent of total national wealth, compared with less than 15 per cent 40 years ago. Third, the poorest own nothing and they now have no support networks – no extended family, no community and no local government to help. Fourth, university education is no longer providing a route towards secure employment and prosperity, as wages for university graduate are declining and graduate-level jobs are becoming precarious. A university degree still gives people a better chance, but it cannot change a more fundamental development: the middle class now earn a lower share of total national wealth than before, while the proportion that goes to the super-rich and the super-super-rich continues to grow.

Fifth, besides economic inequality and differences in power, there is also the growing discrepancy in terms of social status as people with vocational qualifications are considered to be inferior compared with university graduates. More fundamentally, liberal meritocracy is the wrong organising principle for societies that value stability and reciprocal recognition, as Michael Young already argued in his book *The Rise of the Meritocracy* published in 1958.[15] That is because it divides people into winners and losers and privileges the public realm over the private sphere even though the latter has primary importance for most of us. The same flaw applies to social mobility today, which accepts that the price for the rise of some will be the fall others rather than instituting different paths towards individual fulfilment and mutual flourishing.

Sixth, markets are not becoming more competitive. Instead, we are seeing more and more private monopolies or cartels that fix prices and extract rents – excess profits that go to the top managements and the institutional shareholders. For example, intellectual property rights – patents, trademarks and copyrights – are now much more important but are in the hands of a small number of big businesses. This has created huge profits for multinational corporations such as pharmaceuticals, hi-tech, biotechnology and many entertainment companies, which now preserve their monopolies longer than ever. It has also meant high prices for average consumers.

Seventh, other corporations benefit from what is called monopsony, which can be defined as the power to dictate wages to workers and prices to suppliers. As a result, businesses now have substantial market dominance, including those owning network portals and platforms (Amazon, Facebook and Google) as well as the largest banks.[16] Moreover, finance now governs capitalism in ways that are dangerous for markets and people. The capitalist system so much depends on creating abstract wealth that it is increasingly unable to generate productive capital and genuine goods serving human needs. One indication is that global finance uses other people's money to trade almost exclusively with itself: taking deposits and lending to industry accounts for only 3 per cent of assets on the balance sheets of UK banks, while international foreign exchange trading is nearly 100 times the volume of commerce in goods and services.[17] The total exposure under derivative contracts is estimated to be $700 trillion – a multiple of the total value of global GDP.

Finally, all these developments have led to an explosion of easy credit and thereby private debt. In turn, this weakens the position of individuals and families, while workers' rights are under threat from transnational businesses. They make employment conditions worse for people by threatening to outsource unless workers agree to lower wages. Given these changes in the structure of capitalism, it is no surprise that corporate profits have increased as a portion of the total US economy, while wages have declined. Those whose income derives directly or indirectly from profits – corporate executives, stock-market traders and shareholders – have done exceedingly well, while those dependent primarily on wages have not.

In short, all the profit goes to the top of the economy while all the risk goes to the bottom of society. Subsidies by central government for corporations taking on debt, together with support for the growth of global finance through deregulation, have helped to generate a bubble economy of boom and bust that brings about significant economic dislocation.[18] This system is neither economically nor politically viable. Popular alienation and anger is already fuelling the anti-establishment revolt, which the process of economic globalisation as part of the liberal world order is reinforcing. All this is exacerbated by mainstream Western political parties and their embrace of variants of progressivism, combining economic with social liberalism.

How identity politics is eroding the West

Arguably, the other element of liberal hubris is cultural. Contemporary liberalism fuses market fundamentalism with social egalitarianism and liberal identity politics. Identity politics focuses on the values of individuals or separate groups rather than on what people share as citizens and what binds them together as members of national communities. By privileging difference over common bonds, it supplants a sense of belonging and shifts the character of politics in four ways: first, from contribution and sacrifice to a culture of victimhood; second, from building a common life to a politics of protest; third, from the struggles of representative democracy to direct action outside parliament; finally, from collective agency to narcissistic group think that is amplified by the echo chambers of social media.

The rise of identity politics marks the triumph of the 1960s motto that "the personal is the political". Since then, liberals on the left and on the right have celebrated the diversity of difference at the expense of civic ties that bind people together above the divides of class, colour, creed, wealth or gender. Freedom to choose applies most of all to the wealthy and powerful who are at home in a world of mobility and permanent change. This implies that cultural traditions and people's sense of belonging are on the "wrong side of history" and will be swept away in the name of progress and aspiration. The loss of a shared national identity and mutual obligations has undermined both social cohesion and civic patriotism, especially in Europe where politics now oscillates between the pursuit of a cosmopolitan utopia and an anti-establishment revolt that often takes the form of nationalism and even ethnocentric atavism.

Liberalism's identitarian turn is also fuelling the flames of the US culture wars and exacerbating the divisions of both parties. The Democrats' embrace of minority groups such as students, middle-class feminists, African-Americans, Hispanics and public sector employees, as well as vested interests on Wall Street and in Silicon Valley, has alienated traditional white working-class supporters who flock to Trump but despise the Republican establishment.[19] Neither party seems capable of building a majority that can begin to unite the country, but for now this is even truer for the Democrats. As Mark Lilla has suggested, "in recent years American liberalism has slipped into a kind of moral panic about racial, gender and sexual identity that has distorted liberalism's message and prevented it from becoming a unifying force capable of governing".[20]

The implications go beyond the US or any other country. Such a politics lacks emphasis on commonality and is unable to capture people's imagination and a sense of shared destiny for citizens within and across Western nations that are at the heart of the liberal world order. Combined with the triumph of corporate crony capitalism, this is not simply weakening the West compared with the state capitalism of China and Russia. It is also changing the fundamental character of Western civilisation from being a cultural community bound together by common values that define shared interests to a "business community" based on sectional interests that promote divisive values, as Susan Strange anticipated in 1990.[21]

Today, liberals patronise or simply ignore those who neither support economic-cultural liberalism nor benefit from its effects. Hillary Clinton's jibe about half of Donald Trump's supporters as a "basket of deplorables" encapsulated the concept of liberal elites for ordinary people. For them as for other voters, free trade, mass immigration and cosmopolitan multiculturalism have meant greater economic hardship and unnerving cultural comprises, which threaten their ways of life. Compared with the emphasis on self-organisation and mutual solidarity in the case of the civil rights movement, the Democrats' embrace of the abstract values of "diversity", "emancipation" and "inclusivity" has promoted an identity politics that is no less divisive than Trump's atavistic nativism because it is a "coalition of the fringes" that excludes the white working class and sections of the middle class who resent identity politics for everyone else but them. Neither the Democrats nor the Republicans in their current configuration have a positive conception of place and belonging around which new alliances can emerge that overcome the old identity politics of the "culture wars".

Increasingly fragmented at home, Western powers lack the cohesion and resolve to defend a broad, generous Western culture abroad. Roger Scruton puts this well: "If all that Western civilization offers is freedom, then it is a civilization bent on its own destruction. Moreover, freedom flaunted in the face of religious prohibitions is an act of aggression, inviting retribution from those whose piety it offends".[22] Indeed, identity liberalism entrenches a sectarian, minority politics at a time when the West requires resolution to build broad alliances. As the commentator Ross Douthat explains, identity politics has been so influential and endemic (especially among the left) precisely because it is partly a reaction against the abstract formalism of procedural liberalism – ground-rules of fairness instead of a substantive conception of justice. Neither strand of the liberal tradition will regain popular trust and win majority support, since

> people have a desire for solidarity that cosmopolitanism does not satisfy, immaterial interests that redistribution cannot meet, a yearning for the sacred that secularism cannot answer [...] A deeper vision than mere liberalism is still required – something like "for God and home and country," as reactionary as that phrase may sound. It *is* reactionary, but then it is precisely older, foundational things that today's liberalism has lost. Until it finds them again, it will face tribalism within its coalition and Trumpism from without, and it will struggle to tame either.[23]

What is at stake is a politics that can reach beyond either individual or group identity to articulate a vision of national renewal that can mobilise new alliances around a sense of shared belonging – the family, work, places people inhabit, love of country and an appreciation of civilisational inheritance.

Nor this is limited to the liberal West. Liberal culture is increasingly about the identical repetition of a generic vacuity masquerading as an endless succession of diversity and difference. This is reflected in the tendency of capitalism towards re-branding essentially the same products and services. More broadly, it can be observed that capitalist culture, especially in the US, is homogenous – despite the extraordinary diversity in origin of its population and the influx of foreign talent. Nevertheless, American mainstream culture deals in abstract, generic and kitsch ideals: "it's amazing to fall in love with a blue-eyed blonde, it's sad to grow old and best to try to avoid it". This kind of low-grade US culture is accessible to all, but it is corrosive of both universal high and particular local folk cultures. For this reason, people outside the US resent it even as they consume it, as the American commentator Christopher Caldwell has argued.[24]

But the problem extends to the rest of the West. Why, Caldwell asks, should a member of a national culture want to get caught up in a European culture "marked as much by self-doubt as by arrogance"? Europe and the wider West have "squandered its religious and moral inheritance on a forced march to modernity". It can offer "no higher ideal of the good life beyond, travel, longevity and consumerism".[25] The reason why this matters for the liberal world order is because the current clash of values opposing the ultra-liberalism of Angela Merkel, Emmanuel Macron and Justin Trudeau to the anti-liberalism of Donald Trump and other insurgents exacerbates divergent interests within the transatlantic alliance and the wider West on issues of free trade, mass immigration, multiculturalism and democracy promotion, which are central to the international system.

The illiberal non-West

In addition to the rejection of liberalism in Western populations, the global backlash against the liberal world order extends to non-Western countries such as Russia and China that oppose Western liberal culture and norms underpinning the international system in the name of their own civili-sational-state model. This model is based on a claim to embody unique cultural, ethnic and familial relationships that encompass communities both at home and abroad, as I will argue in Chapter 3 in more detail. In the case of civilisational states, the sphere of influence is not simply a means to greater geoeconomic and geopolitical power but also an end in itself – the affirmation of a geocultural identity that gives rise to a distinct voice in the world. On the Eurasian continent, these rival spheres of influence intersect and collide – both between the Western liberal and the Eastern conservative civilisations, but also between Russia and China, where rival identities and narratives compete for loyalty from Central Asian and South Caucasian states.

On the face of it, the illiberal non-West is thriving. China's rise seems inexorable, as Beijing grows increasingly assertive and restless in its pursuit of national interest and a distinct civilising mission – a neo-Confucian pro-ject of harmonious development in the "Middle Kingdom" and its orbit.[26] Under Xi Jinping's leadership, China is developing a global network that combines access to resources and market outlets with political leverage, especially along the new silk roads and in Africa.[27] However, the Chinese

Communist Party leadership is tightening its grip on power at home in response to fears that the country's rapid economic development might lead to greater demands for political reforms. Moreover, Beijing also encounters growing resistance in its own "backyard" in relation to its activities in the East and the South China Sea but also further afield in Africa, where local protests against China's economic exploitation are on the rise, for example, in countries such as Zambia.

Similarly, the Moscow-led Eurasian Economic Union (EEU) is expanding and now encompasses five members: Armenia, Belarus, Kazakhstan, Kyrgyzstan and Russia. The Kremlin enjoys its new-found foreign policy clout in the Middle East and has invested billions in a far-reaching programme of military modernisation that has been tested on the battlefield in the Donbass and especially in Syria. But in reality, the EEU lacks economic vibrancy and political cohesion, as it relies on resource exports and is dominated by Russia's interests, which often diverge from those of its neighbours. While institutional consolidation has given Russian-led Eurasia greater visibility alongside the US, China and the EU, the area is stuck in a geopolitical grey zone between East and West. This is illustrated by Russia's ambivalent relationship as a non-Western power in strategic and institutional terms but with Western cultural orientations and social aspirations.[28] Russia's own pivot to Asia has opened up some opportunities, but by the same token, it leaves the country more dependent on Beijing, which views Moscow at best as a junior partner and at worst as a quasi-vassal state.

Under President Erdogan, Turkey has long harboured ambitions of leadership on an equal footing with the European West. Its strategic location at the interface of Europe, Asia and the Middle East makes the country an indispensable interlocutor for Brussels, and it has built an "axis of convenience" with Moscow that reflects a shared non-Western outlook. But Turkey's attempt to engineer regime change in Syria, combined with its ambivalent stance vis-à-vis ISIS and Sunni fundamentalism, has cast doubt over its basic commitment to the Western alliance. An increasingly authoritarian Ankara will all but rule out Turkey's membership of the EU and creates the potential for conflict with NATO members, not least the Trump Administration.

In terms of East-West relations, there have been two dominant developments over the past decade. On the Western side, there is a strengthening of the Atlantic outlook through an effective convergence between the EU and NATO and thus a new phase in Atlanticism compared with the EU's attempts after 1989 to carve out an autonomous role. This has strengthened the liberal world order in the short-term but made it even more dependent on US leadership in the long-term, leaving it vulnerable when the US retreats (as seems to be case under Trump) and Europe is unable and perhaps even unwilling to step up – whatever Angela Merkel's and Emmanuel Macron's ambition to strengthen the EU's external border and upgrade its defence identity.[29]

On the Russian side, there is a greater Eurasian outlook. Moscow has reinforced ties with non-Western powers such as China (through the Shanghai Cooperation Organization) and Turkey, thus inaugurating a new phase in Eurasianism compared with Boris Yeltsin's attempts to integrate Russia into the West in the early 1990s. Taken together, these developments mark the abandonment (for now) of a Greater Europe where all European powers can act together. The "new Atlanticism" and the "new Eurasianism" leave the liberal world order divided along similar lines compared with the Cold War. The former precludes an independent EU and the creation of autonomous strategic capabilities that would enable the Union to become a global actor in its own right, while the latter cements Russia's outsider status in relation to the West in institutional and strategic terms.[30]

This new East-West confrontation reinforces the resolve of the illiberal non-West, which has been increasingly assertive for the past decade or so. The first systematic expression of Russia's non-Western orientation was given by President Putin in his speech at the 2007 Munich security conference, in which he accused the US of plunging the world into chaos by warmongering, meddling in other countries' affairs and disregarding international law. More specifically, Russia adopted an anti-Western stance insofar as it rejected the geopolitical reality of the Atlantic West as a putative hegemon on account of a list of grievances: first, EU and NATO expansion and the moving of the frontiers of both blocs to Russia's borders, combined with the deployment of an anti-ballistic missile defence shield as a further sign of encircling Russia's Western part; second, the West's aggressive promotion of democracy and human rights in ways that bring about regime change and support overly anti-Russian governments in the shared neighbourhood; third, regime change in Afghanistan and Iraq (later followed by Libya) without UN authorisation and thus in contravention of international law. At the heart of this critique lies a rejection of US exceptionalism and EU tutelage, which Moscow associates strongly with a Western claim to universality on which the liberal world order ultimately rests.

In response to the breakdown of strategic relations with the West for the past ten years, Moscow has not so much rebuilt the Soviet Union or recreated the Tsarist Empire as reconstituted its military power and reasserted its foreign policy influence worldwide. The Kremlin has not rejected the entire post-1945 or post-1989 order (with its territorial arrangements and normative premises), but it seeks a balance of power that recognises Russia's claim to be an equal in that system and a country with legitimate national interests. In turn, this has led to an increasingly assertive approach to foreign policy and international affairs, starting with the opposition to the 2003 Iraq invasion, the pushback against the colour revolutions and the Russo-Georgian war, and more recently followed by the annexation of Crimea, the incursion into Ukraine and the intervention in Syria. Allied to this is the vast modernisation of Russia's armed forces, the upgrading of military capabilities and a turn away from Western models of development towards a more Eurasian path – including conservative values, traditional representations of state sovereignty and a multipolar international system that is supposed to replace the unipolar liberal world order dominated by the US.[31] After two decades of US unipolarity and the "end of history" idea of a global convergence to Western market democracy, rival cultural values and civilisations are coming again to the fore of geopolitics.

In conclusion of this chapter: the Anglophone liberal empire is still the globe's most potent coalition, but its hegemony is unravelling because it lacks a coherent intellectual vision and the necessary cultural-social cohesion. For today we have, instead, a distinct shift back to a more nakedly interest-based foreign policy and, above all, to "great power games" and spheres of influence[32] – a dynamic that accounts in large part for the beginning of a deep freeze in Europe in the wake of the Ukrainian crisis and continual conflict in the Near East. Thus, we are witnessing the return of a Westphalian geopolitics, albeit in a mutated form, that revives and accentuates its inter-imperial dimension in terms of geoeconomics and a global "culture war" between Western liberalism and its adversaries.

However, this is not the end of the liberal world order because economic liberalism, which is one of its pillars, has gone global. There is an oscillation between anarchy and order, which reinforces the market-state in the West and the state-market in China, Russia and India – market capitalism or state capitalism but capitalism either way. Just as Trump fuses protectionism with "neoliberalism in one country", so China champions liberal globalisation without political liberalism in order to promote "socialism with Chinese characteristics" – including a raft of protectionist, mercantilist and predatory policies. In other words, we are seeing the emergence of paradoxical polarities – the "market-state" of the liberal West and the "state-market" of the illiberal non-West (as in the case of China and to a lesser extent Russia). The point is that the post-1989 liberal world order is unravelling and the post-war system in retreat, which represents a fundamental challenge to the previous hegemony of Western liberalism.

Notes

1 Ivan Krastev, 'The Unraveling of the Post-1989 Order', *Journal of Democracy*, Vol. 27, no. 4 (October 2016), pp. 5–15; Jan Zielonka, *Counter-Revolution. Liberal Europe in Retreat* (Oxford: Oxford University Press, 2018).
2 Thomas Wright, 'Trump's 19th-century Foreign Policy', *Politico* Magazine 20 January 2016, at www.politico.com/magazine/story/2016/01/donald-trump-foreign-policy-213546?paginate=false
3 Vladimir Putin has described the purpose of the Eurasian Union in the following terms: "The Eurasian Union is a project for maintaining the identity of nations in the historical Eurasian space in a new century and in a new world. Eurasian integration is a chance for the entire post-Soviet space to become an independent centre for global development, rather than remaining on the outskirts of Europe and Asia", in remarks at the Meeting of the Valdai International Discussion Club, Novgorod, 19 September 2013, full transcript online at http://en.kremlin.ru/events/president/news/19243
4 Anne Applebaum, 'Even if Trump Loses, the "Populist International" Wins', *Washington Post*, 7 November 2016; John Lloyd, 'The new Illiberal International', *The New Statesman*, 20 July 2018, online at www.newstatesman.com/world/2018/07/new-illiberal-international
5 Jamie Bartlett, 'Italy's Five Star Movement and the Triumph of Digital Populism', *The Spectator*'s Coffee House blog, 5 March 2018, online at https://blogs.spectator.co.uk/2018/03/italys-five-star-movement-and-the-triumph-of-digital-populism/
6 Anthony Barnett, 'Corporate Populism and Partyless Democracy', *New Left Review*, 3 (May–June 2000), pp. 80–89.
7 C.B. Macpherson, *The Political Theory of Possessive Individualism: Hobbes to Locke* (Oxford: Clarendon Press, 1962).
8 Cas Mudde and Cristóbal Rovira Kaltwasser, *Populism: A Very Short Introduction* (Oxford: Oxford University Press, 2017), p. 116.
9 Nick Lowles and Anthony Painter, 'Fear and Hope – The New Politics of Identity' (London: Searchlight Trust, 2011), available online at www.fearand-hope.org.uk/project-report; Laurent Bouvet, *L'insécurité culturelle. Sortir du malaise identitaire français* (Paris: Editions Fayard, 2015).
10 Erik Brynjolfsson and Andrew McAfee, *The Second Machine Age: Work, Progress, and Prosperity in a Time of Brilliant Technologies* (New York: Norton, 2014).
11 Thomas Piketty, *Le capital au XXIe siècle* (Paris: Seuil, 2013), trans. *Capital in the Twenty-First Century*, tr. Arthur Goldhammer (Cambridge, MA: Harvard University Press, 2014).
12 Robert Reich, 'Friction is Now Between Global Financial Elite and the Rest of Us', *The Guardian*, 11 November 2015, available online at www.theguardian.com/commentisfree/2015/nov/11/us-uk-politics-economics
13 Edward Alden, *Failure to Adjust: How Americans Got Left Behind in the Global Economy* (Lanham, MD: Rowman & Littlefield, 2017); Richard V. Reeves, *Dream Hoarders: How the American Upper Middle Class Is Leaving Everyone Else in the Dust, Why that Is a Problem, and What to Do About It* (Washington, DC: Brookings Institution, 2017).
14 Reich, 'Friction Is Now Between Global Financial Elite and the Rest of Us', *op. cit.*

15 Michael Young, *The Rise of the Meritocracy* (London: Thames and Hudson, 1958); 'Down with Meritocracy', *The Guardian*, 29 June 2001, available online at www.theguardian.com/politics/2001/jun/29/comment

16 Barry C. Lynn, *End of the Line: The Rise and Coming Fall of the Global Corporation* (New York: Doubleday, 2005); *Cornered: The New Monopoly Capitalism and the Economics of Destruction* (Hoboken: John Wiley & Sons, 2010).

17 John Kay, *Other People's Money: Masters of the Universe or Servants of the People?* (London: Profile, 2015), pp. 80–140.

18 Brink Lindsey and Steven Teles, *The Captured Economy: How the Powerful Become Richer, Slow Down Growth, and Increase Inequality* (New York: Oxford University Press, 2017).

19 Joan C. Williams, *White Working Class: Overcoming Class Cluelessness in America* (Boston: Harvard Business Review Press, 2017).

20 Mark Lilla, 'The End of Identity Liberalism', *New York Times*, 18 November 2016, available online at www.nytimes.com/2016/11/20/opinion/sunday/the-end-of-identity-liberalism.html?_r=0, expanded as *The Once and Future Liberal. After Identity Politics* (New York: HarperCollins, 2017).

21 Susan Strange, 'The Name of the Game', in Nicholas X. Rizopoulous (ed.), *Sea Changes: American Foreign Policy in a World Transformed* (New York: Council on Foreign Relations Press, 1990), pp. 260–273.

22 Roger Scruton, *The West and the Rest: Globalisation and the Terrorist Threat* (London: Continuum, 2005), p. viii.

23 Ross Douthat, 'The Crisis for Liberalism', *New York Times*, 19 November 2016, available online at www.nytimes.com/2016/11/20/opinion/sunday/the-crisis-for-liberalism.html

24 Christopher Caldwell, 'Gangnam Stylishly Debunks US Myth', *The Financial Times*, 28 December 2012, available online at www.ft.com/cms/s/0/8c831b72-4a16-11e2-a7b1-00144feab49a.html

25 Christopher Caldwell, 'The French, Coming Apart', *City Journal*, Spring 2017, available online at www.city-journal.org/html/french-coming-apart-15125.html

26 Daniel Bell, *China's New Confucianism, Politics in Everyday Life in a Changing Society* (Princeton, NJ: Princeton University Press, 2000); Q. Yaqing, 'The Possibility and Inevitability of a Chinese School of International Relations Theory', in *China Orders the World: Normative Soft Power and Foreign Policy*, ed. W. A. Callahan and E. Barabantseva (Washington, DC: Johns Hopkins University Press, 2011), pp. 30–48.

27 Peter Frankopan, *The Silk Roads: A New History of the World* (London: Bloomsbury, 2015).

28 Richard Sakwa, 'How the Eurasian Elites Envisage the Role of the EEU in Global Perspective', *European Politics and Society* Vol. 17, supplement 1 (2016), pp. 4–22.

29 Adrian Pabst, 'Europe's Commonwealth: Greater Europe Beyond Core EU and Economic Eurasia', in Peter Schulze (ed.), *Core Europe and/or Greater Eurasia: Options for the future* (Frankfurt/New York: Campus, 2017), pp. 71–93.

30 Richard Sakwa, *Russia against the Rest: The Post-Cold War Crisis of World Order* (Cambridge: Cambridge University Press, 2017).

31 Marlène Laruelle, 'Russia as an Anti-Liberal European Civilisation', in *The New Russian Nationalism, 2000–15*, edited by P. Kolstø and H. Blakkisrud (Edinburgh: Edinburgh University Press, 2016), pp. 275–297.

32 John Mearsheimer, 'Why the Ukraine Crisis Is the West's Fault: The Liberal Delusions that Provoked Putin', *Foreign Affairs*, Vol. 93, no. 5 (2014), pp. 77–89; Richard Sakwa, *Frontline Ukraine: Crisis in the Borderlands* (London: I.B. Tauris, 2014).

3　Interregnum

The battle for hegemony

Liberal interregnum

The global revolt against liberalism bears the hallmarks of what the Italian philosopher Antonio Gramsci called "interregnum". First of all, the Brexit vote and the victory of Donald Trump, as well as the growing support for far-left and far-right parties across the West, highlight the collapse of the authority of the political class and the common sense that underpinned political domination. In Gramsci's words, "If the ruling class has lost consensus, that is, if it no longer 'leads' but only 'rules' – it possesses sheer coercive power – this actually means that the great masses have become detached from traditional ideologies".[1] Second, the crisis of authority points to a wider, conjunctural crisis: "The crisis consists precisely in the fact that the old is dying and the new cannot be born; in this interregnum morbid phenomena of the most varied kind come to pass".[2] These morbid phenomena are not limited to the ultra-liberalism of Justin Trudeau and, to a lesser extent, Angela Merkel and Emmanuel Macron but include the political extremes of Donald Trump, Nigel Farage and Beppe Grillo's Five Star Movement, as well as the ruling ideologies in the countries of the illiberal non-West, such as Russia, Turkey, India and China.

Third, the anti-liberal insurgency has put liberals on the back foot or even dislodged them from power (as in the US and Italy), but it has not and likely will not defeat liberalism altogether. The reason for Gramsci is that there are deeper, organic trends – historical forces – which shape the conjuncture, the interregnum, and the new settlement that will eventually emerge:

> A crisis occurs, sometimes lasting for decades. This exceptional duration means that incurable structural contradictions have revealed themselves (reached maturity), and that despite this, the political forces which are struggling to conserve and defend the existing structure are making every effort to cure them, within certain limits, and to overcome them.[3]

In other words, liberalism will keep on reinventing itself and fight back in order to reassert its dominant, if not hegemonic, position. The liberal world order has not been dislodged and the forces supporting it are among the most powerful interests across the West.

But in a deliberate inversion of Gramsci's argument, my contention is that it is in reality the new which is dead and the old which is yet to be reborn. The failure of liberalism means that we are witnessing the death throes of liberal humanitarianism and neo-conservatism – and their shared commitment to unfettered economic globalisation, mass immigration and democracy promotion by military means that have come to characterise the liberal world order. The death of the new marks the end of the liberal "hegemony", the defining Gramscian idea that conceptualises political domination beyond the state and the market into the realm of culture and society – the norms and values underpinning the liberal world order. As Gramsci argued, the interregnum is a time when politics has to shift from a "war of movement" to a "war of position". Whereas a "war of movement" is fought on existing (nowadays liberal) terms of debate, a "war of position" is a battle over the very purpose of politics and the creation of a new order – and the international system is at present in just such an interregnum.

The liberalism that informs the international system is not about to dis-appear and the main institutional pillars of the liberal world order will likely endure. But as a philosophy and a governing ideology, liberalism is caught up in an irresolvable contradiction. It promises release from any constraint not chosen by consenting individuals who are portrayed as having no obli-gations to anyone while simultaneously being increasingly subordinate to an overweening state and the unfettered free market.[4] Here one can go further to suggest that liberalism goes against the grain of humanity and erodes the cultural foundations on which it rests.[5] The triumph of liberal international-ism more and more brings about the "war of all against all" (Hobbes) and the idea of man as self-owning animal (Locke) that were its assumptions. But this does not thereby prove those assumptions, because – as the French philosopher Jean-Claude Michéa has suggested – it is only *really existing* liberalism that has produced in practice the reality that it originally assumed in theory.[6] In this way, liberalism represents the unnecessary victory of vice over virtue – of selfishness, greed, suspicion and coercive control over com-mon benefit, generosity, a measure of trust and persuasive power.

Today, the failure of liberalism is clear to see. Just as liberal thought redefines human nature as fundamentally individual and abstracted from social embeddedness, so too liberal practice replaces the quest for recipro-cal recognition and mutual flourishing with the pursuit of wealth, power and pleasure – thereby contributing to economic insecurity, cultural disorder, ecological devastation and international anarchy. Even careful defenders of liberalism, such as the *Financial Times* columnist Edward Luce, acknowl-edge that the crisis of liberal politics is "real, structural, and likely to per-sist" because Western elites cling to a conceit about the primacy of Western thought and refuse to "admit that the West has no monopoly on truth or virtue".[7]

Liberalism is no longer hegemonic but it remains the default position of (former) mainstream politics, which no longer commands majority support because the adoption of social-cultural and economic liberalism has undone post-war coalitions between working-class and middle-class people that were once the foundation of the post-war consensus on which the liberal world order depended. In North America and Europe, the two main parties converged around a liberal economics of free trade, low corporation tax, the primacy of shareholder interest, winner-takes-all compensation, financial liberalisation, rationalised welfare and restrictions on organised labour. This led to a process of financialisation, de-industrialisation and corporate glo-balisation that reinforced an economy of low wages, low productivity, low innovation, industrial decline, job-exporting trade deals and bail-outs for banks "too big to fail" without transforming banking or looking after those who lost their homes and struggled with debt.

The ruling elites have lost or are on the back foot because to economic liberals the non-metropolitan areas are uncompetitive, inefficient and in need of "market correction", while for social liberals, working-class cul-tures cling to a past long gone and to backward values that will be swept away by a bright new cosmopolitan future. Neither on the ground of eco-nomic interest nor of social identity could left and right liberals find any reason to defend working-class communities. The popular revolt against the hitherto dominant Davos dogma at the heart of the liberal world order opens up a space in which a new "war of position" is fought. One dimension of that "war of position" is the battle for hegemony between the ideology of ultra-liberalism that is ruling but no longer leading, on the one hand, and its ideological rivals, on the other – in particular, the emerging ideology of nationalist traditionalism that shapes much of the illiberal (non)-West.[8] Another dimension is the battle for hegemony between the defenders of the liberal world order and the advocates of alternatives arrangements – includ-ing a resurgent contest between "great powers".

"Great power" resurgence

How to conceptualise "great powers" and imperial politics in an age when the liberal world order is in crisis? A useful starting point is the early work of the English School, in particular the writings of Martin Wight who makes the general point that the shape of international relations is not like a timeless law of nature but rather influenced by specific cultural traditions. More specifically, different cultures shape the principles and practices that make up geopolitics and the exercise of power. One corollary is that sovereign equality is an abstract ideal, which fails to capture the various degrees of sovereignty that characterise individual states and different international systems – including suzerain state-systems.[9] Adam Watson has developed this line of thinking by expanding the spectrum of possibilities ranging from independence at one end via hegemony and suzerainty to dominion and absolute empire at the other end. Since the extremes at both ends are usually unstable, most international systems tend towards the middle, i.e. variants of suzerain power with concentric circles – direct authority over a core, with a periphery of locally autonomous rulers who recognise overlordship and pay tribute, and units that are domestically independent but constrained in terms of their foreign policy as well as units recognised as independent but not equal because the Suzerain is of a different, "great power" or even globally hegemonic, order.[10]

Such a conceptual picture can capture a number of characteristics that mark out the US, China, Russia and the EU and relations with the countries in their respective sphere of influence. For example, the Monroe Doctrine means that Washington has tended to take military action against any regime in its backyard that is deemed to be hostile to the US and poses a threat to US domination. Similarly, Moscow and Beijing behave like suzerain powers vis-à-vis a number of neighbouring countries with which they entertain asymmetric relations analogous to lords and vassals – security in exchange for political loyalty and market access. As Ole Wæver has argued, suzerain systems are radial in nature and have gradated forms of imperial power. Here, the notion "imperial" or "empire" is used in a metaphorical sense to denote a centre that not only has more power than the periphery but also projects influence through cultural attraction.[11] In this sense, "empires" involve a measure of universalism and hierarchy, though not necessarily to the point of declaring peripheral units as wholly unequal, "other" and uncivilised. Such exceptionalism only applies to complete, universalist "meta-empires" such as Rome and China in Antiquity or European colonial powers and the Soviet Union in the modern era.[12]

"Great powers" – conceptualised as suzerains – and "imperial politics" – conceptualised as a mix of geopolitical, geoeconomic and "geocultural" influence – are different from categories such as *Reich* and *Grossraum* in the work of Carl Schmitt who, as Ola Tunander notes, generalised the legal norms of the US Monroe Doctrine to suggest that formally independent nations can only survive by being subordinate to an empire that operates based on the friend-foe logic.[13] According to Schmitt, a "greater space" (*Grossraum*) denotes a cluster of states with a high degree of economic interdependence and with a central imperial power (*Reich*) that secures order by preventing external military intervention. Some form of dialogue with the foe – the "Other" – is possible precisely because the friend-foe logic recognises difference, whereas for Schmitt, the universalism of liberal and Marxist ideology reduces the foe to a "learner" who must abide by the standards of civilisation before he can be admitted to the club of the elect.[14] But by contrast with Schmitt's focus on the natural condition of anarchy and the logic of inevitable conflict in geopolitics, the above conception of "great powers" and "imperial politics" suggests that there is a pre-established order and that suzerains with gradated forms of power can coexist precisely because they often have spheres of influence with partially overlapping cultures. Today, for instance, the EU, Turkey and Russia and their partly shared neighbourhood have certain European cultural traditions in common even if the nature of these ties is debated and the claim by Ankara and Moscow to be European is contested (including by domestic political forces).

Thus, it can be argued that the English School in the tradition of Wight and Watson (rather than Bull and his disciples) develops in a more culturalist direction notions of "great power" and "imperial politics" that are central to the writings on geopolitics by Halford Mackinder and Rudolf Kjellén at the beginning of the twentieth century.[15] Common to both is the idea of cultural divides, which is far less prominent in the work of Schmitt or Karl Haushofer who understood culture in terms of nature as a struggle between biological units – individuals and nations – that follows the logic of Social Darwinism.[16] Mackinder and Kjellén, on the contrary, viewed cultural divides as constitutive of geopolitics. Mackinder distinguished sea-based Atlantic powers from land-based continental powers, combining geographic and spatial notions such as "pivot zone" and "heartland" with cultural traditions, while Kjellén opposed Russian and English universalism to German-Slavic multicultural cosmopolitanism. Whether or not the detail of these ideas is correct or not, what matters for the purposes of my argument is the focus on "great cultural divides" that continue to shape geopolitics: first of all, the divide between Russia and the (Atlantic) West; second, the divide between Orthodox Christians and Muslim Turkic populations (and its implications for the relations between the two "great powers" of Russia and Turkey in Central Asia); third, the divide between Germanic Europe and Latin Europe (and its consequences for the Eurozone and the unity of the EU as a "great power").

As Wight would say, "great powers" can be conceptualised as "the Great Responsibles".[17] They are seldom loved and often feared, as Machiavelli might put it, and they do override the interest of smaller states in their quest for domination and hegemonic power. But by the same token, they can also provide stability and a measure of order through common interest. For both Wight and Herbert Butterfield, common interests are historically and culturally contingent and therefore subject to a great deal of change. But at the same time, there is a certain permanence that has to do with cultural ties, which often cross borders and territories. Against the Hobbesian fear of a violent state of nature and the "war of all against all" and also against Rousseau's bleak choice between "a state of war" and a "troubled peace", Wight and Butterfield emphasise the social nature of humankind and the idea that human cooperation precedes the contractual arrangements both within and across nations. Just as national societies are bound together by much more than contracts, so too the international society of states is governed by a set of customs and traditions that are more fundamental than either formal rights or commercial exchange.

Precisely in the absence of a single sovereign who wields coercive power, the glue that most of all holds together societies both nationally and internationally is "an antecedent common culture", which is more primary than the rights of individual citizens or the authority of sovereign states.[18] Culture so configured rests on a shared "cosmic, moral constitution" that is metaphysical in nature because it links immanent values to their transcendent origin and outlook.[19] Examples include the dignity of the person or the equality of all people beyond differences of colour, class and creed. In this manner, the early writings of the English School shifts the focus away from unilateral practices centred on self-interest and individual entitlements towards more reciprocal arrangements that rest on the balance between rights and responsibilities – what Wight called the link between "common interest" and "common obligation".[20] This argument develops Wight's fundamental point that in modernity "[s]overeignty had indeed passed to different states, by social contracts, but the original unity of the human race survived".[21] Thus, international society embodies the common interests and values, as well as the common rules and institutions that bind states together and qualify notions of state sovereignty. But one question that arises from this is whether the English School views international society in more statist or more cultural terms. This, in turn, raises a further question about culture and civilisation in the liberal world order. An important dimension of the global backlash against liberalism is the celebration by powers such as China, India or Russia of their civilisation and their conviction that global stability depends upon coexistence and mutual respect of civilisational identity.

The rise of civilisational states

It is commonplace to assume that China and Russia are national states as they can be defined in terms of a circumscribed territory with a dominant nation and the institutions of modern statehood. However, in both countries, the nation-state model is associated with the West and its promotion of supposedly universal values, which are seen as Western liberal values that do not reflect the distinct character of Chinese and Russian civilisation. Russia and China can be described as civilisational states in the sense of states that embody, defend and promote a certain civilisation with a focus on ethnic, cultural and ideological identity and cohesion.[22] One reason for characterising them in these terms is because this is part of their own self-understanding and captures the way their political leadership – past and present – sees their country and the differences with the West.[23]

For example, the China expert Martin Jacques reflects this when he compares the nation-state model with the civilisational-state model:

> The most fundamental defining features of China today, and which give the Chinese their sense of identity, emanate not from the last century when China has called itself a nation-state but from the previous two millennia when it can be best described as a civilization-state: the relationship between the state and society, a very distinctive notion of the family, ancestral worship, Confucian values, the network of personal relationships that we call *guanxi*, Chinese food and the traditions that surround it, and, of course, the Chinese language with its unusual relationship between the written and spoken form.[24]

This is not to suggest that the idea of civilisational states is objectively true or has necessarily greater legitimacy than the nation-state model. In fact, both are characterised by internal tensions and contradictions. The nation-state oscillates between protecting national sovereignty and projecting power and influence over the sovereign affairs of other countries – hence the relevance of the concept of spheres of influence in analysing the actions of nation-states such as the US. Similarly, the civilisational state is based on culture, ethnic and familial relationships, which are meant to encompass communities both at home and abroad (diaspora), but which may not have the wider appeal that the term "civilisation" often implies. This raises questions about whether Chinese or Russian civilisation have the capacity to attract many non-Chinese and non-Russian people.

These questions arise from the way in which China's and Russia's current political leadership uses the concept of civilisation in order to strengthen their own legitimacy and their state power both at home and abroad. Xi Jinping links the historical legacy of Chinese civilisation with a certain story about Chinese identity today – what he calls the "Chinese dream". In a speech to UNESCO in the early years of his presidency, Xi put it in the following terms:

> The Chinese people are striving to fulfil the *Chinese dream* [which] is about prosperity of the country, rejuvenation of the nation, and

happiness of the people. *It reflects both the ideal of the Chinese people today and our time-honored tradition to seek constant progress* … In the Chinese civilization, people's cultural pursuit has always been part of their life and social ideals. So the realization of the Chinese dream is a process of both material and cultural development. As China continues to make economic and social progress, the Chinese civilization will keep pace with the times and acquire greater vitality.[25]

In other words, the Chinese dream is nothing new. It flows, so Xi's argument goes, from a millennia-old history that each generation inherited from the previous one and transmitted to the next. The core meaning of this history is what Xi in the same speech describes as the yearning "for a world of great harmony in which people are free from want and following a high moral standard". Therefore, he claims that China will only attain the promise of the Chinese dream if it puts in place a model of balanced development – the "Beijing consensus" of state capitalism as opposed to the "Washington consensus" of market capitalism – and combines material with cultural progress.

If this can be achieved, then China will be able to take its rightful place among world civilisations, which Xi envisions as follows:

> As we pursue the Chinese dream, the Chinese people will encourage creative shifts and innovative development of the Chinese civilization in keeping with the progress of the times. We need to inject new vitality into the Chinese civilization by energizing all cultural elements that *transcend time, space and national borders and that possess both perpetual appeal and current value* … In this way, the Chinese civilization, together with the rich and colourful civilizations created by the people of other countries, will provide mankind with the right cultural guidance and strong motivation.[26]

Here are the roots of Xi's conception of China's sphere of influence – a civilisational state whose culture transcends "national borders" and is of both "perpetual appeal and current value". This vision underpins China's soft power policy of establishing over 700 Confucius Institutes that are embedded in many universities across the globe, national editions of the official newspaper *The China Daily*, as well as the news agency Xin Hua and China Central Television with its multilingual programmes.

Put differently, China is engaged not simply in geopolitics and geoeconomics but also in geoculture. Like Western countries, it pursues a civilising mission, which it calls "global harmony". This Confucian ideal not just binds domestic politics and international relations together. It also expresses a certain Chinese exceptionalism that gives rise to an idea of international order and influence beyond national borders[27] – i.e. the possibility of becoming a hegemon with a sphere of influence. Unlike Western colonialism, China's leadership will embody the "Way of Humane Authority" that reflects the country's peaceful rise and its long history of opposing "foreign barbaric foes".[28]

So the form the Chinese geocultural sphere of influence takes is that of a supposedly "harmonious world order" in which Beijing aims to play a preeminent role. In his speech at the opening ceremony of the 19th Communist Party Congress of China in October 2017, Xi said this: "It will be an era that sees China moving closer to centre stage and making greater contributions to mankind ... The development of China is no threat to any other country. No matter how much China has developed, it will never seek hegemony or expansion".[29] Thus, the Chinese civilisational state preserves China's unique model based on cultural characteristics without striving for some unipolar domination over the rest of the world.

For its part, Moscow also appeals to the idea of civilisational state as a source of legitimacy and a greater Russian role in the international order. In his annual "state of the union" address in 2012, Vladimir Putin declared that "for centuries, Russia developed as a multi-ethnic nation ... a civilisation-state bonded by the Russian people, Russian language and Russian culture ... uniting us and preventing us from dissolving in this diverse world".[30] And in remarks to an audience of Russian and foreign experts in 2013, he defined Russia as a "state-civilisation" in the following terms:

> Russia – as philosopher Konstantin Leontyev vividly put it – has always evolved in "blossoming complexity" as a state-civilisation, reinforced by the Russian people, Russian language, Russian culture, Russian Orthodox Church and the country's other traditional religions. It is precisely the state-civilisation model that has shaped our state polity. It has always sought to flexibly accommodate the ethnic and religious specificity of particular territories, ensuring diversity in unity.[31]

Seen in isolation, these words appear to be mere statements about Russian history and culture. However, President Putin has linked this reading of the historic evolution of the Russian state to the creation of the Eurasian Economic Union (EEU) – his flagship foreign policy project since returning to the presidency in 2012, which is an expression of Russia's sphere of influence. In the same remarks to the group of experts, he described the EEU as a project that combines unity with diversity – almost like an extension of Russia:

> The Eurasian Union is a project for maintaining the identity of nations in the historical Eurasian space in a new century and in a new world.

> Eurasian integration is a chance for the entire post-Soviet space to become an independent centre for global development, rather than remaining on the outskirts of Europe and Asia. I want to stress that Eurasian integration will also be built on the principle of *diversity*. This is a *union* where everyone maintains their identity, their distinctive character and their political independence. ... We expect that it will become our common input into maintaining diversity and stable global development.[32]

Like Xi, Putin believes that the liberal values associated with the West are not universal and do not capture the civilisational identity of Russia and the neighbouring countries in the post-Soviet space. Russia's self-definition as a civilisational state provides the Kremlin with a justification to intervene in the affairs of the "near abroad" on grounds of a shared civilisation that extends to the Russian diaspora.[33] This is based not just on historical grounds but also the continued presence of so-called "co-patriots" – people of Russian descent who have ties of affinity with Russia and have been left outside of Russian borders since the dissolution of the Soviet Union.[34]

These are not new themes in Russian geopolitical thinking. Already in 2008, the Russian Foreign Minister Sergey Lavrov spoke of the "civilisational unity" of all the lands that used to constitute the Soviet Union and before that the Russian Empire.[35] In the same year, the then President Dmitry Medvedev laid claim to a "sphere of privileged interest", which for him translates into an obligation on the part of the Russian state to defend Russian people abroad.[36] There are some subtle yet significant differences between these two statements of Russian foreign policy. Medvedev put the emphasis on "zones of interests" rather than "spheres of influence". Lavrov, in contrast, is much closer to Putin's accentuation of civilisational ties that underpin Russia's role in the "near abroad" – a sphere of influence in all but name. Far from being merely semantic, the former is about Russia's more specific and identifiable interests that are non-exclusive with other countries' interests[37] – such as the mutual benefits from trade or good neighbourly relations. By contrast, the latter is both all-inclusive and exclusive: first of all, it is coterminous with an idea of international order in which Russia is a "great power" alongside the US and China; second, within this order, Russia exercises influence over countries in the post-Soviet space, which encompasses geopolitical, geoeconomic and geocultural aspects and which excludes other powers (notably the US and the EU) from a strategic area such as Eurasia. The Eurasian continent is moving once again to the fore of global politics in ways that challenge the domination of the liberal world order.

The Eurasian crucible

After the bipolarity of the Cold War and the brief period of US unipolarity, Eurasia is now moving to the centre of international relations as a crucible of geopolitics.[38] In a long tradition dating back to the earliest Western geopolitical thinkers Mackinder and Kjellén, the Eurasian space can be seen as the heartland of global geopolitics where the fate of empires old and new is determined. This focus on land power rather than sea power led Mackinder to formulate the dictum for which he is best remembered: "Who rules East Europe commands the Heartland. Who rules the Heartland commands the World-Island [Eurasia]. Who rules the World-Island commands the World".[39] In one sense, Eurasia can be considered as the chessboard of the world where a new "great power" game is in full swing and rival spheres of influence intersect and collide. But in another sense, Eurasia can also be considered as a bridge between East and West – a continental connector from China via Russia and the Middle East to Europe and the Atlantic West, including North America.[40]

In either case there are not only geopolitical and geoeconomic drivers but also and perhaps increasingly geocultural forces at work, which are not captured by the "end of history" thesis of a global convergence towards Western liberal democracy or by the "clash of civilizations" between the West and "the rest". Rather, the contemporary contest over power in Eurasia highlights the cultural dimensions of the rival spheres of influence, above all, China's Neo-Confucian "One Belt, One Road" initiative and Russia's creation of the Eurasian Economic Union as a concrete expression of the "Russian world" (*Russkiy mir*). In both cases, the current political leadership of China and Russia view their civilisational-state model not simply in instrumental terms as a means to greater political power and economic wealth, but as an alternative to the US nation-state model and the European cultural commonwealth, which are associated with liberal values that are seen as sources of instability, decline and conflict.

China's "One Belt, One Road" project aims to bring about profound economic and political changes in Eurasia and Africa based on certain ideas about Chinese culture, civilisation and world history along the Silk Road. It rests on a broad framework of what Beijing describes as cooperation and connectivity, which encompasses the coordination of policy, the pooling of investment and people-to-people bonds. Far from simply enhancing economic prosperity and political power, China deploys heritage diplomacy in order to help rebuild a rich cultural legacy that is supposed to connect present Chinese society to its past and also draw other peoples into China's wider orbit – including 34 UNESCO world heritage sites. This is part of fostering Chinese civilisational identity at home and abroad, which reflects

Beijing's strategy of using culture as a source of international influence. Among numerous examples there is the Silk Road programme, which represents an ambitious attempt to achieve the first rank in the global table of UNESCO heritage properties by preserving over 500 sites and thereby overtaking Italy. Therefore, culture is a reason in its own right and it also serves the purpose of further extending China's sphere of influence. This sphere is rooted in, and deepens, a long history of cultural interactions between China and other countries in Eurasia, and it operates as bridge between heritage sites, which directly align with Beijing's trade and foreign policy ambitions.

From a Chinese point of view, the Silk Road programme offers key neighbouring countries a place in an expanding Sino-centric network of power, wealth and status: one cultural corridor linking China with Mongolia and Russia; another Eurasian land corridor all the way from Beijing to Brussels; yet another corridor consolidating ties between China and Pakistan with its strategically important port of Gwadar close to the Persian Gulf. Based on the Neo-Confucian idea of harmony, the Chinese leadership wants other countries to find points of cultural connection through the rebuilding of share heritage sites led by China, which is a way to pursue regional influence and forge ties of loyalty. Both by land and sea, the "One Belt, One Road" initiative with its focus on Silk Road heritage diplomacy is a multi-annual project of fostering both institutional and interpersonal bonds that tie other cultures to Chinese civilisation.

The stated ambition of the Chinese leadership is not simply to project geoeconomic power and military might but also to create what Xi Jinping has called a "Community of Common Destiny" that is non-hegemonic precisely because it rests on new international structures (such as the Asian Infrastructure Investment Bank or the Shanghai Cooperation Organization) that are not dominated by Western powers. As China demands a role that is commensurate to the size of its military and economy in shaping this region, one way to conceptualise this growing assertiveness is in terms of a civilisational state at its centre and an expanding sphere of influence that focuses on non-Western culture as a pole of attraction to other Eurasian countries – including Russia, Mongolia, the five Central Asian republics, Pakistan and Afghanistan. Thus, geoculture complements geopolitics and geoeconomics by aiming to bring about a more permanent realignment away from the US and the EU towards China.

Up to a point, Russia under President Putin pursues a similarly non-Western path insofar as Moscow no longer (as in the 1990s and early 2000s) seeks integration with the West. Instead, the Kremlin lays claim a role on par with that of the US in a multipolar world and is engaged in consolidating links with countries independently of Western institutions. This includes the Collective Security Treaty Organization, the Shanghai

Cooperation Organization and the Eurasian Economic Union. Key to this project is the idea of a "Russian world" (*Russkiy mir*) that consists of all Russian-speaking peoples inside and outside of Russia's borders. The word "world" is used in the sense of a civilisational space (Greek or Byzantine "world") with a dominant civilisation at the centre and a concentric circle of peripheries with diverse degrees of political loyalty and economic integration.[41] *Russkiy mir* is a geocultural notion that underpins a geopolitical imagination of Russia's global standing on par with other "great powers" – as a distinct civilisation that is anti-liberal yet also European with which different regions of the world have diverse links.[42]

Like China's invocation of Neo-Confucian "harmony", *Russkiy mir* is both an end in itself (Russia's self-understanding and projection of a specific Russian voice in geopolitics) and a means to a greater projection of power (a legitimation for maintaining and fostering a sphere of influence in the "near abroad" and beyond). As a result, *Russkiy mir* reconnects the country with its pre-Soviet and Soviet past and suggests an unbroken continuity in Russian history of which the civilisational state is the ultimate guarantor. The creation of the *Russkiy Mir* Foundation in 2007 and its cultural centres abroad is a concrete expression of this vision and of the Kremlin's efforts to promote both Russian language and culture across the globe, as is the establishment in 2008 of *Rossotrudnichestvo* – the Federal Agency for the Commonwealth of Independent States, Compatriots Living Abroad and International Humanitarian Cooperation. Both were responses to the so-called "colour revolutions" in Georgia (2003), Ukraine (2004–2005) and elsewhere, which are seen as bitter defeats for the Kremlin that prompted a geopolitical rethink in the form of military modernisation and public diplomacy around reinvigorated spheres of influence.[43]

Thus one function of Russia's diplomacy and cultural policy is the reconciliation with the worldwide Russian diaspora, starting with the people in former Soviet states. This is why Moscow speaks of the post-Soviet space as her "sphere of privileged interests". Even in the formulation of the former President and current Prime Minister Medvedev, this sphere – while potentially open to other countries – is historically and culturally Russo-centric:

> there are regions in which Russia has privileged interests. These regions are home to countries with which we share special historical relations and are bound together as friends and good neighbours ... It is not even a matter of belonging to this or that organisation, this or that bloc, but rather the common history and genetic connectedness of our economies and the very close kinship of our souls.[44]

Whether Medvedev's more open or Putin's more exclusive vision, the point is that Moscow see itself in the role of the balancer between East and West precisely because Russia is a separate civilisation that is neither Eastern nor Western but rather both at once and therefore exceptional – a blend of European with Eurasian values that is at the global centre of gravity and can mediate between the different world civilisations of China, India and the Atlantic West.

This blurriness is not limited to *Russkiy mir* but also applies to the EEU – Putin's flagship foreign policy since returning to the Kremlin in 2012 after serving for four years as Prime Minister. The EEU rests on the idea that Russia's sphere of influence is a projection of the country as the leader and pivot-point of Eurasia in ways which somewhat mirror Mackinder's argument. After the failure of the Commonwealth of Independent States (CIS) and the fragmentation of ties with countries that do not wish to belong to the Russian world (the Baltic States, Ukraine, Georgia and Moldova), Moscow realised that it can only secure its global status as a major power if it is the dominant transregional power on the Eurasian continent. Such a position cannot be purely based on historical grounds but requires a fusion of geo-cultural with geoeconomic influence in order to leverage geopolitical power. Hence the idea, which underpins the creation of the EEU, of reinforcing synergies with neighbouring economies in terms of transit, agriculture and energy.[45] From the Kremlin's point of view, this is the most promising way of countering growing Chinese influence in Eurasia and interventions by the US and the EU while at the same time being open to working with any of them in ways that make Russian an indispensable "partner".

This view shapes the Kremlin's strategy of dealing primarily with other "great powers" beyond its "sphere of privileged interest", which acts as a buffer zone against unwanted foreign meddling in wider Russian affairs. First of all, the US when it comes to the Iranian nuclear deal, until the Trump Administration pulled out; at which point, Moscow vowed to continue cooperation with the leading EU powers, Germany and France; second, Iran and more recently Turkey in relation to the civil war in Syria; third, Germany, France and, to a lesser extent, Italy, concerning the conflict in Ukraine – not least because they belong to a certain continental European tradition that is much more Russophile than Anglo-Saxon Europe with its allies in Poland and the Baltic States.

Finally and most importantly, the EEU is a way for Russia to strengthen ties with China on a shared agenda of countering what the leadership of the two countries view as US arrogance and unipolarity. Both oppose the liberal world order and US and, to a lesser extent EU, interference in the internal affairs of sovereign states through a policy of sanctions and regime change. Moscow and Beijing also want to weaken and ultimately remove Western domination of international organisations such as the IMF, the World Bank and the World Trade Organization by advocating new rules that reflect both the interests and the values of non-Western countries. Their respective sphere of influence is both a buffer zone against what they consider to be Western meddling and a forward position from which to project more power based on conservative cultural visions, which are markedly different from the West's liberal agenda in terms of traditional values of family, patriotism, respect for the authority of the older generation and the state, as well as indigenous religion.

However, there are also tensions between Russia's and China's spheres of influence. One source is power in the Eurasian heartland of the Central Asian republics where Moscow views the growing Chinese presence with some suspicion while Beijing defends what it sees as legitimate political and economic interests precisely because of historical cultural ties. That is why China has opened Confucius Institutes in Russia, Ukraine, the Central Asian countries and the South Caucasus. So far, Russia retains her pre-eminent position but Moscow fears that demographic decline and China's long-term plan will limit and even push back the Russian sphere of influence. The other source of tension concerns the international order. While Moscow has engaged in a more confrontational course against Western economic sanctions and military interventions, Beijing continues to prefer a more gradualist approach.

So far, the Sino-Russian cooperation is based on mutual interests and a broadly shared anti-liberal agenda, but over time, the shift in the global balance of power in favour of China could trigger a Russian response – even a pivot back from the currently more Asian to a previously more Western outlook. The point is that Russian's self-identification as a European-Eurasian civilisational state and Chinese's self-understanding as Neo-Confucian civilisational state encompass spheres of influence that collide not just with those of the US and the EU but also with each other. Eurasia may not be Mackinder's "World-Island" from which to rule the globe, but it is returning to the centre of international relations.

Notes

1 Antonio Gramsci, 'The Third Notebook (1930), §34', in *Prison Notebooks*, ed. and tr. Joseph A. Buttigieg (New York: Columbia Press, 19962), Vol. 2, p. 32.
2 *Ibid.*, pp. 32–33.
3 *Ibid.*, 'Fourth Notebook', §38, p. 177.
4 Patrick J. Deneen, *Why Liberalism Failed* (New Haven, CT: Yale University Press, 2018).
5 John Milbank and Adrian Pabst, *The Politics of Virtue: Post-liberalism and the Human Future* (London: Rowman & Littlefield, 2016), pp. 1–9 and 13–67.

6 Jean-Claude Michéa, *L'empire du moindre mal. Essai sur la civilisation libérale* (Paris: Editions Climats, 2007), trans. *The Realm of Lesser Evil: An Essay on Liberal Civilisation*, tr. David Fernbach (Cambridge: Polity Press, 2009).

7 Edward Luce, *The Retreat of Western Liberalism* (London: Little, Brown, 2017), p. 16.

8 On these new ideological battle lines, see Adrian Pabst, '"War of Position": Liberal Interregnum and the Emergent Ideologies', *Telos*, no. 183 (Summer 2018), pp. 169–201.

9 Martin Wight, 'Western Values in International Relations', in Herbert Butterfield and Martin Wight (eds.), *Diplomatic Investigations: Essays in the Theory of International Politics* (London: George Allen & Unwin 1966), pp. 89–131; Martin Wight, *Systems of States* (Leicester: Leicester University Press 1977). For a comprehensive overview of spheres of influence and the English School, see Hast, *Spheres of Influence in International Relations*, esp. pp. 1–75.

10 Adam Watson, *The Evolution of International Society* (London: Routledge 1992), esp. pp. 122–125.

11 Ole Wæver, 'Imperial Metaphors: Emerging European Analogies to Pre-Nation-State Imperial Systems', in Ole Tunander, Pavel Baev and V.I. Einangel (eds.), *Geopolitics in Post-Wall Europe* (London: Sage Publications 1997), pp. 59–93.

12 Walter Scheidel (ed.), *Rome and China: Comparative Perspectives on Ancient World Empires* (Oxford: Oxford University Press, 2009).

13 Ola Tunander, 'Post-Cold War Europe: Synthesis of a Bipolar Friend-Foe Structure and a Hierarchic Cosmos-Chaos Structure?', in Tunander, Baev and Einangel, *Geopolitics in Post-Wall Europe*, pp. 17–44.

14 Carl Schmitt, *Völkerrechtliche Grossraumordnung mit Interventionsverbot für Raumfremde Mächte – Ein Beitrag zum Reichsbegriff im Völkerrecht* (Berlin: Deutscher Rechtsverlag 1941).

15 Halford J. Mackinder, 'The Geographical Pivot of History', *The Geographical Society*, Vol. 23, No. 4 (April 1904): 421–437; *Democratic Ideals and Reality. A Study in the Politics of Reconstruction* (New York: Holt 1919); Rudolf Kjellén, *Statens som livsform* [*The State as a Living Organism*] (Stockholm: Hugo Gebers Förlag 1916).

16 Karl Haushofer, *Bausteine der Geopolitik* (Berlin: Kurt Vowinckel 1928); *Geopolitische Grundlagen* (Berlin: Spaeth & Linde 1939).

17 Martin Wight, *Power Politics*, 2nd ed., Hedley Bull and Carsten Holbraad (eds.) (Leicester: Leicester University Press, 1995), pp. 43–44.

18 Herbert Butterfield, 'The Historic States System', unpublished paper, quoted in Adam Watson, 'Foreword', in James Der Derian (ed.), *International Theory: Critical Investigations* (Houndsmill: Macmillan, 1995), p. x.

19 Martin Wight, *International Theory: The Three Traditions*, Brian Porter and Gabriele Wight (eds.) (Leicester: Leicester University Press, 1991), pp. 13–14.

20 Wight, *Power Politics*, pp. 293–294.

21 Wight, *International Theory*, p. 38.

22 Christopher Coker, *The Rise of the Civilizational State* (Cambridge: Polity Press, 2019). I am indebted to the author for sharing with me an early draft of the book manuscript and for illuminating conversations over many years.

23 Alastair Campbell, *Defining China's 'Civilization State'. Where is it heading?* (Sydney: China Study Centre, 2015), Policy Paper Series, online at https://sydney.edu.au/china-studies-centre/our-research/centre-publications.html; Margaret Light, 'Russian Foreign Policy Themes in Official Documents and

Speeches: Tracing Continuity and Change', in Margaret Light (ed.), *Russia's Foreign Policy Ideas, Domestic Politics and External Relations* (London: Palgrave Macmillan, 2015), pp. 13–29; Fabian Linde, 'State Civilisation: The Statist Core of Vladimir Putin's Civilisational Discourse and Its Implications for Russian Foreign Policy', *Politics in Central Europe*, Vol. 12, no. 1 (2016), pp. 21–35.

24 Martin Jacques, 'Civilization State Versus Nation-State', *Süddeutsche Zeitung*, 15 January 2011, pp. 11–13, online at www.martinjacques.com/articles/civilizat ion-state-versus-nation-state-2/

25 Xi Jinping, Speech at UNESCO Headquarters Paris, 27 March 2014, online at www.fmprc.gov.cn/mfa _eng/wjdt_665585/jyjh (my italics).

26 *Ibid.* (my italics).

27 Feng Zhang, 'The Rise of Chinese Exceptionalism in International Relations', *European Journal of International Relations*, Vol. 19, no. 2 (2011), pp. 305–328.

28 William A. Callahan, *China: the Pessoptomist Nation* (New York: Oxford University Press, 2010); Jiang Qing, *A Confucian Constitutional Order: How China's Ancient Past Can Shape Its Political Future*, tr. Edmund Ryden (Princeton, NJ: Princeton University Press, 2012); Henry Curtis, 'Constructing Cooperation: Chinese Ontological Security Seeking in the South China Sea Dispute', *Journal of Borderland Studies*, Vol. 31, no. 4 (2016), pp. 537–549.

29 Xi Jinping, Address to the 19th Communist Party Congress, 18 October 2017, online at www.chinadaily.com.cn/china/19thcpcnationalcongress/2017-10/18/content_33398037.htm

30 Vladimir Putin, Address to the Federal Assembly, Moscow, 12 December 2012, online at http://en.kremlin.ru/events/president/news/17118

31 Vladimir Putin, Remarks at the Meeting of the Valdai International Discussion Club, Novgorod, Russia, 19 September 2013, online at http://en.kremlin.ru/even ts/president/news/19243

32 *Ibid.* (my italics).

33 Andrei Tsygankov, 'Crafting the State-Civilization: Vladimir Putin's Turn to Distinct Values', *Problems of Post-Communism* Vol. 63, no. 3 (2016), pp. 146–158.

34 Linde, 'State civilisation'.

35 Sergey Lavrov, 'Russia and the World in the 21st Century', *Russia in Global Affairs*, Vol. 3 (2008), online at http://eng.globalaffairs.ru/number/n_11291; Russian Foreign Policy and the New Quality of the Geopolitical Situation, Ministry of Foreign Affairs of Russia, 29 December 2008, online at /www.mid. ru/brp_4.nsf/e78a48070f128a7b43256999005bcbb3/bc2150e49dad6a04c325 752e0036e93f?

36 Dmitry Medvedev, Transcript of interview given to TV channels Rossia, Channel One and NTV, 31 August 2008, online at www.kremlin.ru/eng/speech es/2008/08/31/1850_type82912type82916_206003.shtml

37 Dmitry Trenin, 'Russia's Spheres of Interest, Not Influence', *The Washington Quarterly*, Vol. 32, no. 4 (2009), pp. 3–22.

38 Anita Sengupta, *Heartlands of Eurasia: The Geopolitics of Political Space* (Lanham, MD: Lexington Books, 2009).

39 Mackinder, 'The Geographical Pivot of History', p. 132.

40 Zbigniew Brzezinski, *The Grand Chessboard: American Primacy and Its Geostrategic Imperatives* (New York: Basic Books, 1997); Jared Diamond, *Guns, Germs and Steel: The Fates of Human Societies* (New York: W.W. Norton, 1997);

Robert E. Bedeski and Niklas. Swanstrom (eds.), *Eurasia's Ascent in Energy and Geopolitics: Rivalry or Partnership for China, Russia, and Central Asia?* (London: Routledge, 2012).

41 Marlène Laruelle, *The 'Russian World': Russia's Soft Power and Geopolitical Imagination* (Washington, DC: Center on Global Interests, 2015).

42 Marlène Laurelle, 'Russia as an Anti-Liberal European Civilisation', in Pål Kolstø and Helge Blakkisrud (eds.), *The New Russian Nationalism, 2000–15* (Edinburgh: Edinburgh University Press, 2016), pp. 275–297.

43 Sinikukka Saari, 'Russia's Post-Orange Revolution Strategies to Increase its Influence in the Former Soviet Republics: Public Diplomacy *po russki*', *Europe-Asia Studies*, Vol. 66, no. 1 (2014), pp. 50–66.

44 Medvedev, interview on 31 August 2008.

45 Laruelle, *The "Russian World"*.

4   Commonwealths
The case for cultural association

Order and culture

Depending on how the nature of the current crisis is conceptualised, the liberal world order will either evolve or dissolve. Those who argue in favour of the former scenario point to the fact that the international society with the United Nations at its head remains the fundamental framework for international relations and global politics. From the Bretton Woods institutions via the United Nations, the Universal Declaration of Human Rights and the Geneva Genocide Convention to NATO and later the General Agreement on Tariffs and Trade, which subsequently became the World Trade Organization (WTO), there is a network of economic governance, international law and normative standards such as R2P that shapes the international system in ways that seem to confirm Hedley Bull's conception of international society.

Building on the work of Bull and other English School writers, Trine Flockhart has theorised the contemporary evolution of international society in terms of a "multi-order world" whereby in the two-level system the rival world orders interact with international society and each struggles for hegemony.[1] According to this conception of the international system, the rival world orders with their particular normative claims challenge and even undermine the primacy of the universal international society – the liberal world order is but one of the orders that vies with the civilisational-state order for domination. As Flockhart notes, "a complex network of 'inter-order' relationships will determine the character of the coming multi-order world".[2] Among the example one could cite in support of Flockhart's thesis are the various regional blocs – NATO, the EU, the Eurasian Economic Union, the Shanghai Cooperation Organization, Mercosur or the African Union. There is certainly disagreement between these blocs on a variety of important questions ranging from UN reform via the Western domination of supranational organisations all the way to the creation of new institutions on non-Western terms, such as the China-led Asian Infrastructure Investment Bank (AIIB) or Beijing's One Belt, One Road initiative.

A number of scholars have characterised these and other developments as either post-Western or anti-hegemonic.[3] Common to such interpretations is the claim that modernity is not a unique Western gift to the world but rather a global project with many sources and numerous manifestations, of which Shmuel Eisenstadt's thesis about "multiple modernities" was one of the earliest articulations.[4] If this true, then the confrontation between the West and "the rest" will neither take the form of an "end of history"-style convergence towards Western liberal market democracy, nor will it be an inevitable "clash of civilisations" as prophesised by Samuel Huntington (or rather a simplified interpretation of his argument). And neither will it result in a contest between fundamental values or philosophies that are mutually incompatible or perhaps even incommensurable. Instead, the ongoing power shift from West to East and North to South is perhaps best understood as an almost natural, organic evolution of world politics in which authority, status and privileged are newly redistributed and allocated to render the existing order fairer and more effective. This is certainly one plausible scenario, and various initiatives – such as the UN Alliance of Civilizations – reflect the commitment to cooperation based on mutual respect.

There is, however, another scenario, which English School ideas help us to identify. It focuses on the clash of culture, values and norms that underpin not just rival world orders but also the overarching international society itself. Not only is the application of key provisions of international law contested: when is it legitimate to overthrow an elected president (compare Western and Russian responses to the overthrow of President Yanukovich in Ukraine and President Morsi in Egypt)? And when is it legitimate to intervene militarily in the domestic affairs of nominally sovereign states (compare Western and Russian responses to the Balkans, Iraq, Libya, Ukraine and Syria)? There is also a growing clash of values both within and across countries in the West and elsewhere – not along the old opposition of left *versus* right or democratic capitalism *versus* totalitarian communism but rather a contest between liberal *versus* conservative or globalist *versus* nativist lines.

In each case (clash of legal norms and of cultural values), the question that arises is about the nature of concepts of "norms" and "values". While there might be well be universal values, it is equally clear that norms differ widely not simply between civilisations but also among cultures within a single civilisation such as that of the wider West – e.g., the balance between liberty and equality under the umbrella of security. How to understand the distinction between norms and values? As the strategic thinker Philip Windsor put it,

> All cultures depend on translating certain underlying values into the norms of social behaviour. For the most part they promptly proceed to confuse the two; so that any criticism of a given social norm is regarded

as an attack on the values, which it is supposed to represent. Yet toleration implies respect for other people's beliefs and values, without necessarily implying that the social norms should be condoned.[5]

Because a norm is cultural expression of a value, a norm is defined in terms of a dialectic with values. As such, norms are related to behaviour but are not regulatory. Norms are not about "regulating" action but instead underpin action because they reflect a specific cultural interpretation of a universal value that is embodied in certain specific practices. If this is true, then it follows that cultures and civilisations share values but differ on norms. This is a key insight as "Great Powers" and other countries seek to find common ground but also learn how to live with difference in a world in which they are increasingly interdependent in some respects but perhaps also increasingly divided in other respects – especially in relation to liberal norms shaping the international order.

Here it is instructive to draw once again on the work of the English School, in particular the question about the source and nature of international order. This goes back to the split between Martin Wight and Hedley Bull. Bull agreed with Wight that states are not the exclusive members of "international society", but his conception tends to accentuate the primacy of states at the level of international order compared with the primacy of social life at the level of world order. Now Bull is equally clear that world order in some important sense precedes international order: "World order is not only wider than international order or order among states, but also more fundamental and primordial than it, and morally prior to it".[6] This presents us with a fundamental problem – the source of world order and how it relates to international order. For Bull, "Within international society order is the consequence of a sense of common interests in the elementary goals of social life".[7] But how to square the primacy of world order with the priority of specific cultural habits – the fact that people are born into different cultures and civilisations? One response is to suggest that particular rules and norms are connected with universal values, so we are back to Philip Windsor's point.

But a deeper problem is that the English School also seems to assume, as Nick Rengger writes, that "it is precisely human artifice and invention that has created international society, though it has often arisen, of course, from circumstances not of humans' own intentional making".[8] Thus, the question is whether rules and norms are created in a voluntarist sense that gives rise to obligations codified in contracts, or whether rules and norms emerge more realistically as part of cultural identities that are both material and ideational. Voluntarism reinforces the power of individuals or sovereign states to invent and institute order, whereas realism highlights the belonging of both people and countries to deeply embedded social ties that cross borders.

Culture is in part socially constructed but also reflects certain material realities. There is a widespread view that nations and countries are predominantly social construction – what Benedict Anderson calls an "imagined community".[9] Cultures are invented, and also reinvented, in representation and the imagination – in books, art, music, film and other popular expressions. However, cultures grow out of customs, traditions, institutions and ways of life that are *also* material. Culture is an inheritance that forms a common life providing people with their principal source of meaning, and a sense of identity and belonging. Individuals inherit their culture, but they also contribute to reimagining and remaking it. The anthropologist Ruth Benedict describes culture as "the raw material of which the individual makes his life" without which "no individual can arrive even at the threshold of his potentialities".[10] The loss of a culture is, a "loss of something that had value equal to that of life itself, the whole fabric of a people's standards and beliefs".[11] In his 1958 essay "Culture is Ordinary", Raymond Williams argues that every human society has its "own shape, its own purposes, its own meanings".[12] These are shared yet also contested and cultural traditions are continual arguments over their meaning precisely because of the importance of a culture of shared meanings and values as the necessary foundation of a polity. This matters at a time when liberalism – as a philosophy, ideology and set of institutions – undermines such shared meanings and ways of life.[13]

It also matters because it points to the interaction of ideational with material forces, which suggests a more unified reality than the old opposition between rationalist and reflectivist approaches in IR theory. In turn, it indicates that cultural association is more primary than states or markets that represent the institutional backbone of the liberal world order. What this reveals is an ontology underpinning liberal internationalism which is based on an even deeper dialectical oscillation than that of the individual versus the collective or the market versus the state. The next two sections will show that the liberal world order is grounded in a perpetual movement between the anarchy in the state of nature and the artifice of the social contract and of the international system (Machiavelli, Hobbes and Kant), to which the alternative is – as I will argue – cultural association (Burke).

Anarchy and artifice

The liberal world order builds on ideas that can be traced to the work of Niccolò Machiavelli, Thomas Hobbes and Immanuel Kant. Already with Machiavelli, vice is more fundamental than virtue because evil has greater ontological and political reality than goodness, and thus the city is characterised by a competition for survival and power. In Machiavelli's

The Prince, it is the exercise of violence and the use of fear that regulates civic life, not the pursuit of peace or the practice of virtue.[14] Connected with the primacy of a violent anarchy is the redefinition of virtue: according to the Florentine philosopher, virtue is the military and political excellence required to achieve and sustain collective independence. Such a conception returns virtue (understood as *virtù*) to its etymological root of male aggressive prowess – not the notion of excellence and the "radical middle" that mediates between extremes, like the virtue of courage that lies somewhere along the line between the vice of cowardice and the vice of recklessness (as for Plato, Aristotle and Cicero). Ultimately, Machiavelli's *virtù* is closer to the ancient conception of moral vice than moral virtue, connected with a sense of heroism. The ethos he advocates can be instilled by a certain controlled maintenance of factional struggle within the city, which serves as a training ground for the combative spirit and prepares the city in the fight against external powers. Thus, this conception of politics assumes a given ontological *agon* – a conflict more primary than any peaceful ontological harmony. This conflict is to be regulated and manipulated but cannot be overcome by alternative arrangements that might mirror more harmonious orderings of reality.

Since human nature is characterised by both vice and the quest for *virtù*, it follows for Machiavelli that competition and conflict are the fundamental givens of international relations. In fact, the external realm of foreign affairs is inherently more threatening than the internal realm of domestic politics precisely because there is an unmediated anarchy between states that only the power of rulers can try to mitigate: for example, in his 1503 treatise *Words To Be Spoken on the Law for Appropriating Money*, Machiavelli writes that "among private individuals laws, contracts, and agreements make them keep faith, but among sovereigns only force can".[15] Whereas at home, rules and institutions limit the personal ambition of the ruler and align it with collective goals, abroad, the defence of the state is free of such constraints. Crucially, the survival and the security of the city are the primary objectives, which not only precede the pursuit of peace but also trump notions of honour and justice: "All means are acceptable when the survival of the state is at stake", which *in extremis* can also legitimate pre-emptive wars of expansion.[16] The international system for Machiavelli therefore reflects an anarchy of competitive states that slides into open conflict unless there is some balance of power. But in either case, the use of violence is the universal norm rather than an exceptional last resort.

If Machiavelli develops his conception in part against the classical and Christian legacy, Hobbes' account of international relations is similarly in line with late medieval thought that rejects much of Antiquity and the high Middle Ages, notably notions of reality as originally and at heart peaceful and only violent because of the irruption of fate or sin. While Hobbes is a realist in the sense of IR theory, it is important to emphasise that he was deeply indebted to late medieval nominalism and voluntarism. Nominalism refers to the claim that universals such as the good are but mental names (*nomina*), which do not exist in reality. Voluntarism means that the will as a guiding principle of human action is more fundamental than reason or the intellect.[17] Hobbes' political philosophy derives from certain strands of Calvinism and in particular the belief that, after the Fall and the irruption of original sin, the world is in a condition of anarchic violence.

It is this belief – and undoubtedly his experience of the English civil war – that shaped Hobbes' conception of the "state of nature". In this state, life is famously described as being "solitary, poor, nasty, brutish and short", which is the case because "man is a wolf to man" (*homo homini lupus*) and there is a "war of all against all" (*bellum omnium contra omnes*).[18] This original threat of violent death does not apply to any specific period in history but instead constitutes a principle that is internal to the state – evident only at the hypothetical moment of its violent dissolution. Nevertheless, it remains the case that Hobbes' nominalist ontology involves a commitment to view anarchic violence as more fundamental than a peaceful ordering of reality.

Hobbes, like Machiavelli, assumes a natural condition of anarchy that cannot be overcome. For this reason, the sage of Malmesbury can only envision the imposition of an artificial order – the commonwealth – that merely regulates the violent "state of nature". It is true that Hobbes makes a distinction between a commonwealth by free, contractual institution and a commonwealth by forceful, violent acquisition. But in either case, the sovereign has supreme power to "give life" or to withdraw it from his subjects. Obedience to Leviathan, much like obedience to the Prince in Machiavelli, is absolute for fear of a violent death.[19] And since man is driven by a fear of violent death and self-interested self-preservation, peace – redefined as the absence of open conflict – can only be enforced through the absolute unmediated authority of Leviathan. Thus, the original anarchy in the "state of nature" can only be regulated by an artificial order based on the fear of Leviathan who rules by dividing society and the body politics into its individual components.

For the same reason, there is no overarching authority at the international level – only warring nations that might agree on instituting the artifice of international society. The asocial, isolated individual in domestic politics translates into asocial and separate states in the international realm where neither law nor morality nor any overarching reason can permanently constrain power. This is defined as the possession of power and the appetite for ever-more power that it begets. Even if Hobbes connected natural law to the law of nations, his philosophy rests on voluntaristic ideas of power and self-help in order to create artificial arrangements – rather than reciprocity and cooperation within more natural bonds of sympathy.[20]

For all the emphasis on cosmopolitan ideas, the starting point of Kant's theory of international politics echoes Hobbes' notion of the "state of nature": "Peoples who have grouped themselves into states may be judged in the same way as individual men living in the state of nature, independent of external law; for they are a standing offence to one another by the very fact that they are neighbours".[21] The absence of a formal legal order implies for Kant that the threat of violence and war is the foundational condition of international relations: "In their external relationship with one another, states, like lawless savages, exist in a condition devoid of right [...] this *condition* is one of war (the right of the stronger), even if there is no actual war or continuous active fighting (i.e. hostilities)".[22]

In a different yet fundamentally compatible mode compared with Hobbes, Kant naturalises violence within the order of being and considers inter-state warfare as a natural mechanism to regulate global anarchy. Thus, internationally as well as nationally, a Kantian politics rests on the idea of asocial sociability: human beings are naturally self-interested and jealous vis-à-vis other human beings, but this eventually engenders some kind of competitive order. War is the process through which antagonism is transformed into stability, with human conflict somehow mirroring natural violence:

> Nature has therefore once again used the incompatibility of human beings, even of great societies and state bodies [...] as a means to seek out in their unavoidable antagonism a condition of tranquillity and safety, i.e. through wars, through the overstrained and never ceasing process of armament for them [...] nature drives them to what reason could have told them even without so much sad experience: namely to go beyond a lawless condition of savages and enter into a federation of nations.[23]

So Kant views warfare as an evil necessary to regulate the original violence that is our fundamental human condition. Only war will lead to the formation, destruction and reconstitution of states until such time that national and international arrangements permit the creation of "cosmopolitan commonwealths".[24]

It is true that Kant, unlike Hobbes, does not want merely to regulate international anarchy. His diagnosis of "lawlessness" provides the key for his aim of creating a global order – a set of law-governed external relations between states that exceed existing international law about which he is very critical because it lacks force and therefore cannot provide a sufficiently robust external constraint on states. A balance of power is similarly too weak to regulate relations between nations. For these reasons, he calls for a worldwide union of states:

> There is only one rational way in which states coexisting with other states can emerge from a lawless condition of pure warfare. Just like individual men, they must renounce their savage and lawless freedom, adapt themselves to public coercive laws and thus form an international state *(civitas gentium)* which would necessarily continue to grow until it embraced all the peoples of the earth.[25]

There are many obstacles to realising such a vision, not least the objection that sovereign states consist of nations that are moral personalities and as such enjoy a freedom, which a world government would undermine. Therefore, Kant opts for the idea of a "federation of peoples" (*Völkerbund*). The exact nature of such a federation varies throughout Kant's writing and there is a tension between a more statist and a more cosmopolitan conception of international relations.[26] But there are at least two constants in Kant's account: first, the primacy of a single, united will that underpin both law and power – an idea that derives from Ockham's late medieval voluntarism of which Kant was perhaps the last exponent;[27] second, a formal account of political association that reflects the contractualist nature of inter-state ties: "it is necessary to establish a federation of peoples [*Völkerbund*] in accordance with the idea of the original social contract, so that state will protect one another against external aggression while refraining from interference in one another's internal disagreement".[28]

Just as his proposed solution to the "state of nature" consists in instituting domestic society, so too his proposed solution to international anarchy consists in creating a federative structure. Both are founded upon the artifice of the social contract that regulates the anarchy in the "state of nature" without ever reconciling natural violence. Thereby nations are bound together merely by formal values such as respect and a nominal commitment to the peaceful resolution of conflict but without any real powers of enforcement and no substantive, shared ends.

Great powers such as the US, China and Russia tend to embrace a more Machiavellian and Hobbesian version of realism, while the EU pursues a more Kantian utopia of cosmopolitanism. Neither is a solid basis for an international order that reflects the primacy of embedded social and cultural ties over formal contractual relations or pure power. It is here that the work of Edmund Burke provides an alternative approach.

The alternative of association

Central to Burke's political philosophy is his conception of human beings as naturally linked to others by bonds of sympathy, which prevents fellow human beings from being "indifferent spectators of almost anything which men can do or suffer".[29] Coupled with the passions of imitation and ambition, sympathy helps produce an order that is not imposed upon some pre-existing chaos but rather emerges from nature and its complex connections with nature. It does so by fusing a concern for others with copying those who excel and can offer virtuous leadership – rather than the selfish pursuit of power and wealth. Even though they are "of a complicated kind", these three passions "branch out into a variety of forms agreeable to that variety of ends they are to serve in the great chain of society".[30] Thus, one key difference between Hobbes' and Kant's idea of social contract and Burke's accentuation of society is that the latter evolves with the grain of humanity. In line with the idea that society forms a chain of being, Burke argues that the natural condition of humankind is social and relational:

> The state of civil society is a state of nature; and much more truly so than a savage and incoherent mode of life. For man is by nature reasonable; and he is never perfectly in his natural state, but when he is placed where reason may be best cultivated, and most predominates.[31]

For Burke, relationality translates into the innate desire of human beings to associate with one another.[32] The primacy of association underpins Burke's conception of community as expressed by his famous invocation of the "little platoons":

> To be attached to the subdivision, to love the little platoon we belong to in society, is the first principle (the germ as it were) of public affections. It is the first link in the series by which we proceed towards a love to our country and to mankind [...] On the principle of this mechanic philosophy [French rationalism], our institutions can never be embodied in persons; so as to create in us love, veneration, admiration, or attachment. But that sort of reason which banishes the affections is incapable of filling their place. These public affections, combined with manners, are required sometimes as supplements, sometime as correctives, always as aids to law.[33]

Burke redefines the body politic as a "community of communities" in ways that limit the power of both the state and the market at home and abroad. Therefore, a truly alternative account to Hobbesian realism and Kantian idealism would reject the claim that international society is fundamentally anarchic – a global "war of all against all" that mirrors the violent "state of nature" at the national level. If there is anarchy and violence in the sphere of international relations, then the reason for Burke is the arbitrary division of humankind into isolated individuals and separate states whose existence is predicated on their sovereign power of dominion. This conception of international relations brings about a self-fulfilling prophecy whereby the premise of a violent state of nature leads to the institution of a logic that exacerbates rather than resolves disagreements: "this artificial Division of Mankind, into separate societies, is a perpetual Source in itself of Hatred and Dissention among them. The Names which distinguish them are enough to blow up Hatred, and Rage".[34] Therefore, the artifice of the sovereign state and the state-centric system reinforce some of humankind's worst inclinations towards egotism, greed, distrust and violence.

However, actual international relations are often not so anarchic because the most primary ties, bonds and connections between human beings tend not to be confined to national borders, but rather are transnational inflections of universal human attributes: language, cultural customs, music, art, literary modes, fashions in manners and dress as well as religious belief and practice: "one reason why different countries do not wage war all the time is the widely diffused sense of shared culture and common sensibility which can stretch even across vast geographical distances".[35] Examples include the British Commonwealth, la *Francophonie*, the association of Ibero-American countries, the African Union, the Organization of American States and the Organisation of Islamic Cooperation.

Long ago, but in the same spirit and against the New Whigs, Burke emphasised cultural association as the most universal mode of human political interaction:

> In the intercourse between nations, we are apt to rely too much on the instrumental part. We lay too much weight upon the formality of treaties and compacts. We do not act much more wisely when we trust to the interests of men as guarantees of their engagements [...]. Men are not tied to one another by papers and seals. They are led to associate by resemblances, by conformities, by sympathies. It is with nations as with individuals. Nothing is so strong a tie of amity between nation and nation as correspondence in laws, customs, manners, and habits of life. They have more than the force of treaties in themselves. They are obligations written in the heart. They approximate men to men, without their knowledge, and sometimes against their intentions. The secret, unseen, but irrefragable bond of habitual intercourse holds them together even when their perverse and litigious nature sets

them to equivocate, scuffle, and fight, about the terms of their written obligations. [...] There have been periods of time in which communities, apparently in peace with each other, have been more perfectly separated than, in later times, many nations in Europe have been in the course of long and bloody wars. The cause must be sought in the similitude throughout of religion, laws, and manners. At bottom, these are all the same. The writers on public law have often called this aggregate of nations a *Commonwealth*. They had reason.[36]

This conception contrasts with the conception of nations as individual egos writ large that are driven by not by intellect and reason but the sheer force of will, as with the idealism of Woodrow Wilson that mirrors Machiavelli's and Hobbes' voluntarism. On the contrary, Burke accentuates the primacy of association over the sovereign power of the individual and of the collective under the aegis of an artificial social contract. In this manner, he inverts the modern priority of rights and contracts by arguing that the mutual moral obligations of interpersonal relations are more primary than abstract, formal and procedural standards imposed for purposes of either state administration or market exchange.

Crucially, this extends to ties across nations and sovereign states, which suggests that a "family of nations and peoples" really can embed the society of states and markets – even if this is not reflected in the currently dominant arrangements of international affairs. One might in this light say that, ever since humans walked the earth and crossed continents, *both* the global and the local are more primary and more originally linked than all the more restricted modes of political organisation lying between them – regions, nations, international organisations or the institutions of global governance.

In accordance with this secondary nature of the political middles, Burke argues that "common-wealths are not physical but moral essences. They are artificial combinations, and, in their proximate efficient cause, the arbitrary productions of the human mind".[37] By "artificial combinations" he means effects of human habit and creativity that blend nature with culture. Another way of expressing this idea is in terms of fusing the order of being with the order of knowing and "making". In this manner, "customs, manners, and habits of life" provide the bonds and ties that infuse the immanent political order with a transcendent, even cosmic outlook – notions of goodness and justice that inform ideas about how to organise common life in society. A Burkean perspective shifts the focus from an artificial commonwealth that coercively regulates natural violence to a natural-cultural commonwealth that can uphold peace beyond conflict based on the principle of association.

For example, faced with the absolutism of the French Revolution that sought to remake society in the image of a new conception of humankind disembedded from culture and custom, Burke argued that

> It [Europe] is virtually one great state having the same basis of general law; with some diversity of provincial customs and local establishments. The nations of Europe have had the very same christian [*sic*] religion, agreeing in the fundamental parts, varying a little in the ceremonies and in the subordinate doctrines. The whole of the polity and œconomy [*sic*] of every country in Europe has been derived from the same sources. It was drawn from the old Germanic or Gothic customary; form the feudal institutions which must be considered as an emanation from that customary; and the whole has been improved and digested into system and discipline by the Roman law [...] From this resemblance in the modes of intercourse, and in the whole form and fashion of life, no citizen in Europe could be altogether an exile in any part of it. There was nothing more than a pleasing variety to recreate and instruct the mind; to enrich the imagination; and to meliorate the heart. When a man travelled or resided for health, pleasure, business or necessity, from his own country, he never felt himself quite abroad.[38]

Of course, cultures in Europe have diverged significantly from each other since Burke wrote these words over 200 years ago. There is no question that the past couple of centuries, which witnessed the rise of nationalism and two world wars, have greatly divided societies and peoples from one another. However, it is also true that common cultural customs were never lost altogether and that the post-1945 process of European reconciliation has once again reinforced a sense of shared European cultural roots. The collapse of the Soviet bloc in 1989 and the dissolution of the USSR offered the same prospect for Central and Eastern Europe, but a united Europe from Lisbon and Limerick to Vladivostok is now a more remote possibility than at any point since the end of the Cold War.[39]

Burke's vision of Europe's "polity of culture" provides an alternative to the view that sovereign states or else sovereign individuals are more primary than the overlapping forms of associations – city- or nation-states (Machiavelli and Hobbes) or a "federation of peoples" (Kant and Rousseau) that oscillates between statist authority and a cosmopolitan abstraction from culture. In the final instance, such a vision is not Eurocentric because Burke repeatedly emphasises the importance of inheritance in all cultural contexts. One of the main reasons for his radical critique of the French Revolution is the revolutionaries' disregard for institutions that are ultimately contingent products of specific historical circumstance – in the words of Burke, they are "the gift of nature or of chance".[40] While there is an element of arbitrary human artifice involved in establishing institutions, it is nonetheless the case that our institutional inheritance should neither be distrusted nor dismissed but cherished and organically improved.

As Ian Hampsher-Monk notes,

> for Burke, the contrast is not (as it is for the radical) between an arbitrary set of institutions and a better, more rational set, but between having the good fortune to possess stable institutions *at all* and the anarchy that we risk from rejecting what "time and chance" have given us. Far from its being the case that stable institutions can be deduced from abstract principles, Burke thought that, in the absence of shared conventions – which only a specific historical culture provides – reason was incapable of deducing any specific arrangements.[41]

Thus, Burke's emphasis is squarely on the pre-eminence of common cultural customs over rational calculations as the final foundation of the primacy of association. In Europe's case, this is based on joint manners and the shared legacy of Greco-Roman law and philosophy as well as Judeo-Christian ethics, but this does not preclude cultural commonalities in the case of other continents or civilisations. On this basis, Burke argues for an account of international relations that differs from Machiavellian-Hobbesian realism and Kantian cosmopolitanism: international forms of association involve shared conventions of statecraft and diplomacy grounded in cultural customs. These give rise to a sense of obligation and a right of intervention in the domestic affairs of sovereign states in order to protect and preserve "commonwealths of culture".

Cultural commonwealths

Burkean cultural commonwealths fuse the autonomy of peoples and nations with substantive assistance in case of need, which reflects local customs and habits and does not override them in the name of abstract standards such as procedural democracy or purely individual rights that leave out mutual obligation. For such abstract standards always fall short of real justice because they bracket the good from the court of public discussion and replace it with ground rules of fairness (John Rawls), rights (Ronald Dworkin) or discursive reason (Jürgen Habermas).[42] Substantive international engagement transcends purely formal alliances that merely share liberal principles in common, as the historian Christopher Dawson already realised in relation to the League of Nations.[43] Such an organisation, like that of the UN since 1945, suffers a double deficit, doubly linked. The merely formal principles prevent it from embodying any substantive vision of political and cultural way of life, while the merely formal concert of powers ensures that it lacks any power of real enforcement. The connection between these two deficits arises because principles by themselves produce no concrete unity or power, while contractual ties divorced from a power of enforcement fails to engender concrete agreement.

For these reasons, the UN has either been paralysed by the veto power of one of the permanent members of the Security Council. Or else the power of the UN has been in reality the power of a single sovereign state – the US since 1989, or in the future, possibly China. That power is a necessary part of international relations and might in theory serve the associative purpose of the international society. But since the end of the Cold War, the US and other Western powers have sought to impose on other countries the formalistic and economistic principles of late modern liberalism rather than the more constitutional and cultural practices of earlier liberal traditions. The West has offered this thin gruel rather than the solid sustenance of a more deeply rooted Western civilisation with which other civilisations might enter into conversation. And since culture and civilisation abhor a vacuum, the formalism is in reality complicit with a debased popular culture that cuts out high culture and folk culture. We are back to Christopher Caldwell's diagnosis that the West suffers from a lack of self-belief in its own best traditions. Instead, Western civilisation now brings about in practice the Hobbesian war of all against all that is the presupposition of the liberal world order in theory.

So in qualification of a Hobbesian and Kantian fear of a violent "state of nature", Burke's ideas help us to shift the focus back onto the social nature of humankind and the idea that human cooperation precedes contractual arrangements within and across nations.[44] Beyond mere free-trade areas or a fantasised world government, the social and cultural fabric that holds together societies both nationally and internationally is more primary than either the rights of individuals or the sovereign power of states or indeed any contract between them. And beyond even natural law, one can ultimately appeal to the principle and practice of love or charity, which complements both power politics and natural law, and which relates the dignity of all people to their shared transcendent origin and finality. The anthropological basis for this appeal lies in the human capacity for virtue, including the social virtues of courage, generosity, loyalty, kindness and sympathy, which humans across different cultures have practiced as part of diverse types of association – the social body that lies at the heart of the body politic.

Liberals will object that the alternative of association clashes with value pluralism in an increasingly diverse world, especially in the late modern context of multiculturalism and the global clash of fanatical faiths. But to suggest that competing values are incommensurable is to assume that different values have equal claim to normative validity and that no hierarchical ordering can be obtained that commands popular assent. In the absence of higher-order universal principles from which particular norms derive their moral character, general values such as freedom, equality and security constitute their own foundation and finality. The problem that they are essentially self-validating. However, no value is valuable in itself or as such, not even ancient liberties or modern human rights. Here, one can go beyond Philip Windsor's distinction between values and norms to suggest that values are valuable because they originate from an "invaluable" source and because they are ordered towards an equally "invaluable" *telos* or end – a transcendent principle that illuminates what is valuable and how it ought to be valued, blending the empirical with the normative. The sanctity of life and the dignity of the human person underpin the principles of liberality like fair detention, a fair trial and *habeas corpus* but also free inquiry, free speech and freedom of conscience that are central to notions of freedom, equality and security but are too often neglected by contemporary institutions and practices, as in relation to the liberalisation of euthanasia or the global war against terror.

A Burkean approach shifts the focus away from unilateral practices centred on self-interest and individual entitlements towards more reciprocal arrangements that rest on the balance between rights and responsibilities – what the English IR scholar Martin Wight called the link between "common interest" and "common obligation".[45] Connected with this are the invocation of the common good and the re-invention of "constitutional corporatism" in a more plural guise against both free-market fundamentalism and state capitalism. The former is individualist whereas the latter is collectivist, to which the real alternative is the principle of "mixed government" and the role of corporate bodies in both the polity and the economy. A non-statist corporatism of the kind advocated by Burke diffuses sovereign power away from the institutions of the central state and the free market by promoting the constitutional recognition and political participation of mediating institutions such as professional associations in both the public and the private sector, manufacturing and trading guilds, cooperatives, trade unions, voluntary organisations, universities and free cities.

The adoption of a Burkean model of cultural commonwealths would promote a plural search for the shared common good and substantive ends that can mediate between the individual and the collective will and thus help bind together members of diverse bodies and polities. Thereby, one can refuse the liberal view that the incommensurability of rival values either necessarily requires (an internationally unforthcoming) central sovereign power to arbitrate conflict, which would likely lead to a tyrannical world government lacking in civic consent and popular participation. Or else it would involve a fragile and unstable *modus vivendi*, which can slide into conflict or even war. Taken together, a commitment to the common good and constitutional corporatism by "great powers" and others could in theory transform the dominant model of neo-liberal globalisation and the underlying abstract cosmopolitan culture. The emphasis on shared substantive ends can correct the liberal fixation either with instrumental and transactional relationships (merely national or international corporate interests) or with procedural ties (abstract rules and regulatory agencies). It helps to shift the focus towards the reality of shared cultural and social bonds that matter more in an increasingly globalised world in which peoples and nations long for a mutual recognition of their own sense of belonging to cultural commonwealths.

Notes

1   Trine Flockhart, 'The Coming Multi-Order World', *Contemporary Security Policy*, Vol. 37, no. 1 (2016), pp. 3–30.
2   *Ibid.*, p. 5.
3   Charles A. Kupchan, *No One's World: The West, The Rising Rest, and the Coming Global Turn* (New York: Oxford University Press 2012); Trine Flockhart, Charles A. Kupchan, Christina Lin, Bartlomiej E. Nowak, Patrick W. Quirk and Lanxin Xiang, *Liberal Order in a Post-Western World* (Washington, DC: Transatlantic Academy, 2014); Oliver Stuenkel, *Post-Western World: How Emerging Powers are Remaking Global Order* (Cambridge: Polity, 2016); Richard Sakwa, *Russia against the Rest: The Post-Cold War Crisis of World Order* (Cambridge: Cambridge University Press, 2017); Robert Silvius, *Culture, Political Economy and Civilisation in a Multipolar World Order* (London: Routledge, 2017).
4   Shmuel N. Eisenstadt, *Patterns of Modernity Beyond the West* (London: Pinter, 1987); 'Multiple Modernities', *Daedalus*, Vol. 129, no. 1 (2000), pp. 1–29.
5   Philip Windsor, 'Cultural Dialogue in Human Rights', in Mats Berdal (ed.), *Studies in International Relations: Essays by Philip Windsor* (Brighton: Sussex Academic Press, 2002), pp. 77–90, quote at p. 86.
6   Bull, *The Anarchical Society*, p. 315, n. 9.
7   *Ibid.*, p. 65, n. 9.
8   Nicholas J. Rengger, *International Relations, Political Theory and the Problem of Order. Beyond International Relations Theory?* (London: Routledge, 2000), p. 79.
9   Benedict Anderson, *Imagined Communities: Reflections on the origins and Spread of Nationalism* (London: Verso 1983).
10 Ruth Benedict, *Patterns of Culture* (London: Houghton Mifflin, 1989 [1934]), p. 181.
11 *Ibid.*, p. 183
12 Raymond Williams, *Culture and Society, 1780–1950* (London: Chatto & Windus, 1958), p. 108.
13 See, for example, Nick Lowles and Anthony Painter, 'Fear and Hope – The New Politics of Identity' (London: Searchlight Trust, 2011), available online at www.fearandhope.org.uk/project-report; Laurent Bouvet, *L'insécurité culturelle. Sortir du malaise identitaire français* (Paris: Editions Fayard, 2015).

14 Niccolò Machiavelli, *The Prince*, ed. Quentin Skinner and Richard Price (Cambridge: Cambridge University Press, 1988), ch. IX–X, XIV and XXI, pp. 34–39, 51–53 and 76–79.
15 Quoted in Marco Cesa, *Machiavelli on International Relations* (Oxford: Oxford University Press, 2004), p. 2.
16 Niccolò Machiavelli, *Discourses on Livy*, tr. Harvey C. Mansfield and Nathan Tarcov (Chicago, IL: The University of Chicago Press, 1996), III, pp. 41–42.
17 Louis Dupré, *Passage to Modernity. An Essay on the Hermeneutics of Nature and Culture* (New Haven, CT: Yale University Press, 1993); Michael A. Gillespie, *The Theological Origins of Modernity* (Chicago, IL: University of Chicago Press, 2008).
18 Thomas Hobbes, *De Cive*, reprint of 1651 edition (Whitefish, MT: Kessinger Publishing, 1994), c.1, XII and XIII, pp. 17-18; *Leviathan or the Matter, Forme and Power of a Commonwealth Ecclesiasticall and Civil*, ed. Michael Oakeshott (Oxford: Basil Blackwell, 1960), I, XIII, p. 82.
19 Hobbes, *Leviathan*, II, XVII–XX, pp. 109–136.
20 Adrian Pabst, 'International Relations and the "Modern" Middle Ages: Rival Theological Theorisations of International Order', in William Bain (ed.), *Medieval Foundations of International Relations* (London: Routledge, 2016), pp. 166–185.
21 Immanuel Kant, 'Perpetual Peace', in H.S. Reiss (ed.), *Kant's Political Writings*, 2nd ed. (Cambridge: Cambridge University Press, 1991), pp. 93–130, quote at p. 102.
22 Immanuel Kant, 'Groundwork for the Metaphysic of Morals', in *Kant's Political Writings*, pp. 131–175, quote at p. 165.
23 Immanuel Kant, 'Idea for a Universal History with a Cosmopolitan Purpose', in *Kant's Political Writings*, pp. 41–53, quote at p. 47.
24 Kant, 'Perpetual Peace', p. 90.
25 *Ibid.*, p. 107.
26 Andrew Hurrell, 'Kant and the Kantian Paradigm in International Relations', *Review of International Studies*, Vol. 16, no. 3 (1990), pp. 183–205.
27 André de Muralt, 'Kant, le dernier occamien: une nouvelle définition de la philosophie moderne', *Revue de Metaphysique et de Morales*, Vol. 80, no. 1 (1975), pp. 32–53.
28 Kant, 'Groundwork for the Metaphysic of Morals', p. 165.
29 Edmund Burke, *A Philosophical Enquiry into the Origin of Our Ideas of the Sublime and Beautiful*, 2nd edition (1759), in Ian Harris (ed.), *Burke: Pre-Revolutionary Writings* (Cambridge: Cambridge University Press, 1993), p. 68.
30 *Ibid.*
31 Edmund Burke, *An Appeal From the New to the Old Whigs, In Consequence of Some Late Discussions in Parliament, Relative to the Reflections on the French Revolution*, 3rd ed. (London: J. Dodsley, 1791), p. 108.
32 See Adrian Pabst, 'Obligations Written in the Heart': The Primacy of Association and the Renewal of Political Theology', *Journal of International Relations and Development*, forthcoming (published online on 15 January 2018), https://doi.org/10.1057/s41268-018-0131-7
33 Edmund Burke, 'Reflections on the Revolution in France', in Ian Hampsher-Monk (ed.), *Burke: Revolutionary Writings* (Cambridge: Cambridge University Press, 2014), pp. 47, 80.

34 Edmund Burke, 'A Vindication of Natural Society: or, A View of the Miseries and Evils sharing to Mankind from every Species of Artificial Society (1757)', in Ian Harris (ed.), *Burke: Pre-Revolutionary Writings* (Cambridge: Cambridge University Press, 1993), pp. 8–57, quote at p. 28.

35 Catherine Pickstock, 'Numbers of Power, Lines of Transition: Metaphysics and the Problem of International Order', *Oxford Journal of Law and Religion* Vol. 2, no. 1 (2012), pp. 72–97, quote at p. 75.

36 Edmund Burke, 'The First *Letter on a Regicide Peace*' (1796), in *Burke: Revolutionary Writings*, pp. 253–334, quote at pp. 316–317.

37 *Ibid.*, p. 293

38 *Ibid.*, p. 317.

39 Adrian Pabst, 'Europe's Commonwealth: Greater Europe Beyond Core EU and Economic Eurasia', in Peter Schulze (ed.), *Core Europe and/or Greater Eurasia: Options for the Future* (Frankfurt/New York: Campus, 2017), pp. 71–93.

40 Burke, *Reflections on the Revolution in France*, p. 161.

41 Ian Hampsher-Monk, 'Introduction', in *Burke: Revolutionary Writings*, p. xxxv.

42 John Rawls, *A Theory of Justice* (Cambridge, MA: Harvard University Press, 1971); Ronald Dworkin, *Taking Rights Seriously* (Cambridge, MA: Harvard University Press, 1977); Jürgen Habermas, *Postmetaphysical Thinking: Between Metaphysics and the Critique of Reason*, tr. W.M. Hohengarten (Cambridge: Polity, 1995).

43 Christopher Dawson, *The Judgement of the Nations* (New York: Sheed and Ward, 1942).

44 John Milbank and Adrian Pabst, *The Politics of Virtue: Post-Liberalism and the Human Future* (London: Rowman & Littlefield International, 2016), pp. 347–378.

45 Martin Wight, *Power Politics*, 2nd ed., edited by Hedley Bull and Carsten Holbraad (Leicester: Leicester University Press, 1995), pp. 293–294.

5 Covenant

The resurgence of civilisation

Liberal empire

The extension of the liberal order from the West hemisphere to the rest of the world after 1989 coincided with a "new world disorder" of genocide, ethnic cleansing, resurgent nationalism and the violent redrawing of borders (for example, in Yugoslavia), which liberal policies often exacerbated.[1] The liberal philosopher Michael Ignatieff described the violence in the Balkans and elsewhere as a barbaric force threatening what he calls "liberal civilization", but this forgets the increasingly illiberal turn of liberals.[2] Their aggressive promotion of democracy in the name of supposedly universal – but in reality narrowly liberal, individualistic – human rights ended up producing illegitimate wars and new dividing lines in the former Yugoslavia and across the post-Soviet space. Far from defending a vision of peace based on reconciliation between former foes (as in the post-war era), late modern liberalism became debased and associated with triumphalism and victors' justice, as in Serbia, Iraq and Libya. Ignatieff and his fellow advocates of "liberal civilization" fail to acknowledge the closing of the liberal mind, to adapt the title of Allan Bloom's book,[3] and the mutation of liberalism into an imperialist creed.

Ever since Wilson and the Weimar years, liberal imperialism has had global ambitions. Whether in the past or at present, the liberal commitment to the empty freedom of private choice involves as its dialectal reverse a totalitarian commitment to unmediated power – of the will or of nature that underpin new variants of Social Darwinism. The result is a perpetual contradiction between release and control: greed and lust require surveillance and intervention, so that the ensuing anarchy does not destroy the artificial order based on market-state dominance. Linked to this is the liberal insistence on formal law, rules and regulations imposed from the top down, while at the same time tolerating and perhaps promoting large criminal consortia, as in the US, Mexico, Russia and China.[4] Both law and lawlessness, as well as state terror and non-state terror, seem to be reciprocally reinforcing through covert collaboration.

The new triple threat of anarchy, crime and terror might be one reason why certain modes of religion are once again resurgent. Based on voluntaristic modes of belief, fundamentalist faiths portray themselves as the source of private salvation. Among the examples are Sunni Islamists, Christian Evangelicals, Hindu nationalists and Buddhist warriors who claim that legitimacy derives from some sort of hidden providential fusion (rather than ethical mediation) between the individual and the collective – the personal and the political. In this manner, essentialised identities, whether religious or racial, compete with ultra-liberal identity politics, as I argued in Chapter 2. But both complement the empty liberal formalism precisely because they do not challenge the fundamental assumptions of capitalism, technology and globalisation. The late modern period, which began during the interwar years, can therefore be understood as the era of liberal empire that converged and colluded with forms of totalitarianism and voluntaristic religion.

The liberal world order is not unique or exceptional in the way advocates such as G. John Ikenberry suggest. Like other political traditions, liberalism tends towards imperial power on three accounts. First, stabilising volatile "backyards", as is the case of US interventions in Central and Latin America or the EU in the Balkans. Second, securing natural resources and market outlets, as with liberal free trade agreements and Western state support for multinationals and tech platforms. Third, pursuing a "civilising mission", for example, the US export of democracy by "hard" and "soft" power or the EU's promotion of human rights and civil society in an attempt to project normative power by syndicating its values worldwide. Implicit in the invention and institution of liberal empire is a claim to the supremacy of liberalism's values. They are assumed to be the only ones that are at once principled and pragmatic – universal in validity and adaptable over time and across space. For liberals, liberalism embodies the best of civilised life, while others view liberal culture as debased, even decadent. All this raises once more the question of civilisation in the international system.

Western civilisation in question

In the aftermath of the Cold War, three theses dominated debate in international relations: First of all, Francis Fukuyama's Hegelian invocation of the "end of history" and the supposed global convergence towards a Western model of liberal market democracy.[5] Second, Samuel Huntington's prophecy of a religiously rooted "clash of civilisations" opposing the West and the rest.[6] Third, the impact of globalisation on geopolitical conflict and the possible shift towards a geoeconomic contest in which economic resources and market outlets matter more than territorial conquest and military con-trol.[7] At a time when the prevailing models of both liberalism and globali-sation are increasingly contested, a myriad of conflicts around the world appear to confirm Huntington's view, but his account is problematic in several respects: for example, are the West and Russia really two separate, opposed civilisations? Or, rather, are they not different cultures belonging to a single civilisation that ultimately derives from the fusion of Greco-Roman philosophy and law with Judeo-Christian ethics?[8] Are the West and Russia not as much bound together as they are divided by their shared history that goes back to the Roman Empire in Rome and Constantinople and encom-passes both wars and peace settlements in 1815, 1919 and 1945? Moreover, Huntington was misguided in assuming that the main fault-line would lie between civilisations when in reality most geopolitical conflicts since 1989 have taken place within civilisations – for instance, the West and Russia, or within Islam, between the Sunnis and the Shias.[9] So one of the merits of Huntington's thesis is to shift the focus back to civilisation and the meaning of the West.

In his 2016 BBC Reith Lectures, the British-born Ghanaian-American thinker Kwame Anthony Appiah argued that the West does not exist and that it is time to abandon the idea of Western civilisation.[10] Appiah's narra-tive goes like this: the notion of the West is often associated with the white people of the Global North as opposed to the people of the Global South, and when it is derived from Christianity, it is defined and directed against Islam. But Appiah goes on to assert that Western civilisation is not in fact fundamentally Christian because Christendom owed much more to pagan Rome and Greece than to scriptural revelation and the faith of the Bible (a claim that defies both historical evidence and philosophical literacy).[11] And even the inheritance of classical Antiquity is something Europe in real-ity received from Islam, which preserved Aristotle's manuscripts (a myth that has been perpetuated but ignores the fact that Aristotle's metaphysics and ethics were read in Greek on Mount Saint-Michel at least half a cen-tury before the Latin translation of Muslim commentary on Greek philoso-phy reached France and Italy via Spain).[12] Thus Europe's Renaissance was largely the result of enlightened Islam, so Appiah claims.

Nor is there a straightforward link between Europe and the West: "the very idea of the 'West', to name a heritage and object of study, doesn't really emerge until the 1890s", writes Appiah, "during a heated era of imperial-ism, and gains broader currency only in the twentieth century".[13] Put dif-ferently, the West derives its identity not from any civilisational inheritance but instead from Western colonialism and the Cold War with its propagan-distic narrative "from Plato to Nato". And so the West's self-delusion is that "Western culture was, at its core, individualistic and democratic and liberty-minded and tolerant and progressive and rational and scientific. Never mind that pre-modern Europe was none of these things".[14] All of Appiah's assertions reveal an astonishing ignorance about late Antiquity and the Middle Ages, which blinds him from seeing the deep continuities with modernity.

There are at least six such continuities that Appiah fails to mention. First, the idea of the dignity of the person and the principle of equality between men and women stem from the Jewish and Christian notion of creation in the image and likeness of a personal Creator God. Second, the notion of individual rights was inherited from Roman and Germanic law and then developed by thirteenth-century canon lawyers. Third, the separation of political from religious authority goes back to Jewish prophets calling kings to standards of justice and righteousness and Greco-Roman ideas of "mixed constitution". And centuries of state-church conflict ended in a certain constitutional balance that created a space for free association and political liberty.[15]

Fourth, the origins of popular and representative democracy and the accountability of rulers to their people lie in late medieval attempts to curtail the power of both absolutist emperors and theocratic popes in favour of more properly constitutional monarchies and greater collegiality within the Church. Fifth, both patristic and medieval theology considered reason and faith to be mutually augmenting whereas by contrast early modern thinkers sundered rationality from belief and thus invented both fideism and rationalism. Sixth, the roots of modernity are traceable to fourteenth-century theologians who repudiated the Greco-Roman logic of necessity and fatalism in favour of the biblical contingency of the created world, with a renewed emphasis on free will and the autonomy of the natural universe.

Appiah's ignorance of Western intellectual and cultural history leads him to reject outright any notion of unity, which he wrongly equates with essentialism, and to assert that the only alternative to essentialist notions of civilisation is a "cosmopolitan picture in which every element of culture – from philosophy to cuisine to the style of bodily movement – is separable in principle from all the others".[16] According to Appiah, culture is little more than a collage available to anyone at will. The implication is that history, tradition and cultural inheritance are devoid of meaning and that people have no bonds of attachment and affection with historical or cultural practices. Only the cosmopolitan culture of late modern liberalism can free us from the Dark Ages in which Western civilisation supposedly holds humankind hostage.

By contrast with Appiah's post-modern conception of identity as fragmented and in endless flux, the historian Niall Ferguson views the rise of the West in decidedly modern terms as the triumph of liberal civilisation.[17]

In many ways, Ferguson's approach is both a complement to Kenneth Clarke's focus on the arts and architecture inherited from the (Holy) Roman Empire on which modern Western society rests,[18] and a corrective to Appiah's claim that high culture never penetrated the everyday lives of ordinary people in the West. By dwelling "more down and dirty than high and mighty", Ferguson's account of civilisation shows how high culture was sustained and spread across countries and their population by the material forces of political, economic and social organisation. What he calls the "six killer apps" are the ideas embodied in institutions and practices that enabled "the West" (Western Europe and North America) to triumph over "the rest" (Asia, Africa and Latin America) over the past 400 years or so: competition, modern science, private property, medicine, the consumer society and the Protestant work ethic.

The point is less about the historical detail than the logic underpinning Ferguson's conception of Western civilisation. Much of his argument is that the West pioneered these interventions and that they are Western achievements that continue to be more entrenched in the cultures of the West as a political community. He acknowledges the debt modern Western civilisation owes to Islam in relation to scientific discoveries and medical progress, but his claim is about the modern institutions spreading the benefits of progress beyond elites to the wider population. Examples include property rights reflecting the rule of law, which also formed the basis of representative government and accountability rather than mere expropriation and enslavement. Ferguson recognises Western crimes at home and abroad, and he rejects any notion of irreversible trends or law-like regularities in history. Nevertheless, his account risks overstating the modern break with earlier history and underplaying the continuities with the past – including the complex connections between the early modern feudal exploitation of land and labour, which together with "enclosures" extracted a surplus that was invested by London merchants in overseas piratical trade by state-backed businesses such as the East India Corporation. In turn, this provided the basis for the capitalist take-off in the mid-to late sixteenth century.[19]

And whereas Appiah attributes the West's achievements largely to Islam, Ferguson credits modern Western civilisation. But either way both of them view history through a liberal lens and therefore do not acknowledge the extent to which liberalism inherited but did not invent the ideas shaping the West. Connected with this is Appiah's and Ferguson's failure to recognise just how interwoven and intertwined civilisations have been from their inception until the present day.

In fact, the Greek origins of the West can themselves be traced to the civilisations of the East, not least because Greece is the crucible of the Mediterranean where the Eastern and Western worlds intersect.[20] This made the Greeks the most Easterly of all Western people – an honour that they bequeathed to Byzantium and then Russia. As Christopher Coker argues, the philosophy of the pre-Socratics with its emphasis on the four elements (earth, water, air and fire) was most likely shaped by Zoroastrianism in the civilisation of Persia, notably the idea that eternal fire symbolises divine wisdom.[21] Just as the Persians worshiped the god Wisdom, so too the notion of *theos* recurred in the surviving fragments of Heraclitus. Given this legacy, it is no coincidence that *sophia* is central to Eastern Orthodoxy and sophiology at the heart of Russian philosophy since the eighteenth century, including the works of Vladimir Solovyov, Pavel Florensky, Sergey Bulgakov, Nikolai Berdyaev, Georges Florovsky and Semen Frank.[22]

Similarly, the roots of Christianity go back not only to Judaism but also to its encounter with Hellenic civilisation following the territorial expansion under Alexander the Great. The fusion of biblical revelation with ancient philosophy did not date from the earliest Christian times but can be traced to those Jewish communities in whose midst emerged Hellenised Judaism. This is perhaps most of all true for Philo of Alexandria (20BC–50AD), who was a contemporary of Jesus and argued for an allegorical interpretation of Scripture that drew on ancient mythology and philosophy – an experience that foreshadowed the "inculturation" of Christianity in pagan societies.[23] This history-changing encounter was ambivalent: on the one hand, among the Jewish people there were those like the Maccabees and the Zealots who opposed any rapprochement with Hellenism and therefore rejected the very idea of Jesus as the Son of God.[24]

But on the other hand, Greek civilisation introduced into Judaism words such as "synagogue" and generated Hellenised traditions in which both Jesus himself and the Apostles were rooted, as were the Apostolic Fathers and the Apologists who viewed Greek (and Roman) philosophy as *preparatio evangelica* – paving the way for Christian centres of learning around the Middle East, North Africa and Europe with scholars from home and abroad. Combined with the Benedict-inspired monastic communities from the sixth century onwards and later the nascent network of universities and schools linked to cathedrals, the rise of Christendom embodied both the ideational and material transformation of Western Antiquity. This "discontinuous continuity" in the civilisational history of the West was perhaps most clearly represented by the millennium-long existence of the Holy Roman Empire.[25]

Besides the epic and lyric poetry that the Romans inherited from Greece, Roman civilisation also developed based on a repeated re-reading of classical literature and philosophy that could be described as a form of "nonidentical repetition" of perennial themes such as the nature of knowledge or the foundation and finality of truth. Christendom (and later the West) increasingly linked inherited ideas, which it refined, to material change in such a way that agency extended beyond elites. The Renaissance and later the Industrial Revolution brought about the change for which Antiquity had many of the tools but of which it lacked a real conception.[26] One source for this was the legacy of the "Axial Age" (the period 800–200BC), in particular the belief in the freedom of human beings whose fate is not pre-determined by the gods. Rather, personal flourishing requires some form of salvation by a benign deity, which rejects sacrificial practices to appease divine wrath and instead represents itself the ultimate guarantor for the irreducible dignity of the person.[27]

Little of this would have happened without other civilisational encounters between Rome, India and China going back many millennia. In addition to the Indo-European language family, West and East had shared roots in the Mesopotamian world during the Bronze Age when the wheel and the plough first emerged.[28] Over time, these complex ties included other key inventions in astronomy (the equatorial system of lunar mansions) and medicine (theories of pneumatic physiology), which developed differently in India, China and Greece. From before the Shang dynasty (1500 BC), there was something like an "essential unity" between Europe and China when it came to scientific discovery in relation to the social development of civilisation.[29] And by 200 BC, East and West had also converged in terms of key aspects of political organisation, including the formation of single empires – the Roman empire and the Han empire – that represented new political and cultural frameworks to unify warring tribes.[30]

Both empires were ruled by "sophisticated elites schooled in Axial thought, living in great cities fed by highly productive farmers and supplied by elaborate trade networks … The expansion of the cores was eating away at the distance between them, folding East and West into a single Eurasian story".[31] Connecting them was the network of Silk Roads – the key artery between the two halves of Eurasia.[32] While there were hostile waves in one direction or the other (Alexander's army marching eastwards, the marauding Mongols westwards), it is equally the case that such forays led to the intermingling of civilisations, for example, the blending of Greek with Indian culture in the case of the kingdom of Batricia in what is now Afghanistan – whose disintegration in 130BC is mentioned in both Eastern and Western documents. Diplomats, merchants and missionaries from China, India and Rome brought hitherto separate civilisations into contact with one other and left their mark. Memories of ambassadorial meetings, foreign coins, religious influence and the DNA of agricultural slaves in southern Italy that can be traced to maternal ancestry in East Asia. These civilisational interactions were both material and ideational, as illustrated by the Greek philosophy of Plato and Aristotle, the Nyaya School in India and the Hundreds Schools of Thought in China that grew out of complex cultural exchanges across the Eurasian continent.[33]

So what might be the contemporary signification of all this for our under-standing of Western civilisation? One way to conceptualise geopolitics today is with the help of political geography. Most writings on globalisation imply that space is compressing to the point where it becomes marginal or even irrelevant but, as Robert Kaplan reminds us, we forget geography at our own peril.[34] In suggesting that the mapping of mountains, rivers and plains deter-mines destiny, Kaplan renews the legacy of late nineteenth and early twen-tieth-century thinkers like Rudolf Kjellén and Halford Mackinder, whose 1904 article "The Geographical Pivot of History" argued that control of the "Eurasian Heartland" would decide who controls the world.[35] While the work of Kjellén and Mackinder has been used to legitimate the racist imperialism of Nazi Germany, the question that their pioneering work on geopolitics raises is the relation of the Euro-Atlantic West to the Eurasian continent.

The tension between the transatlantic alliance as a political commu-nity and the wider West as a civilisational community is intensifying at the same time when geopolitical and geoeconomic power is shifting from the Atlantic world to Eurasia where the "rising powers" of China, India and Russia are vying for influence and strategic leverage. The West is increas-ingly split between President Trump's US that is retreating from Europe and the Middle East to focus on the Asia-Pacific Rimland, and the EU led by Chancellor Merkel that focuses on its wider neighbourhood (Eastern Europe, the Balkans and the Mediterranean) in the knowledge that it can no longer depend on American protection. Both are largely absent from Eurasia and therefore from what Mackinder thought was the centre of geo-politics: in his memorable words, "Who rules East Europe commands the Heartland. Who rules the Heartland commands the World-Island [Eurasia]. Who rules the World-Island commands the World".[36] It is unsurprising that the divisions and decline of the West coincide with a growing Western absence from the Eurasian continent where Russia and China are locked in a "great power" contest for hegemony.

More than a hundred years after Spengler prophesised the demise of the Occident (*der Untergang des Abendlandes*),[37] the US remains the sole superpower and NATO the only military alliance with a global reach. But the "revenge of geography" raises fundamental questions about whether in world historical terms the Atlantic Age marked the beginning of a new norm represented by the Westphalian system of sovereign states and global markets or rather an exception to the rule of empires, city-states and trans-national religious networks.[38] If it is the former, the weakening of the West can be reversed within a Western-dominated liberal world order. But if it is the latter, then the resurgence of China, Russia and India might herald a pendulum shift back to Eurasia and the making of another, non-Western world order.[39]

The liberal order versus Western civilisation

At the heart of the liberal world order lies the West and at the heart of West lies a paradox: compared with civilisational states such as contemporary China or Russia, the West is the only civilisational community of nations and peoples founded upon shared political values rather than a predominantly national history.[40] Those values are the self-determination of nations, the self-government of people, democracy and free trade, which were codified by the 1941 Atlantic Charter and later enshrined in the post-war international system. Yet at the same time, the West as a political civilisation and the liberal world order it has since then underwritten erode the foundations of Western civilisation and thereby weaken the West's ability to confront both internal problems and external threats – including economic injustice, social fragmentation, resurgent nationalism, ecological devastation, Islamic terrorism and the rise of Eastern authoritarian state capitalism led by China. Davos-driven cartel capitalism, divisive identity politics, rampant secularisation and the legacy of liberal/neo-conservative interventionism are hollowing out Western folk culture and high culture and weakening its global standing. As a "liberal civilisation", the West's political community undermines the common cultural customs, belief and practices of its nations and peoples, as well as the intellectual, literary and artistic achievements that have made the West a distinct civilisation. In this sense, the West is its own *first* enemy.

In turn, this casts doubt on the dominant liberal conception of civilisation, which rests on three questionable assumptions. The first is that civilisational identity is either fragmented and in constant flux or fixed and immutable. The second is that civilisations are either the product of other civilisations to which they owe most of their supposed achievements or self-contained and untouched by others. And the third is that civilisations are either arbitrary arrangements of fact and fiction that mask a lack of coherence or purpose except the pursuit of power and wealth or else that there is a single cultural code, which connects a civilisation's essential identity to its social norms. Underpinning these seemingly opposed presuppositions is a false dualism between the modern era and what preceded it.[41] Modernity collapses a series of dyadic relations such as nature and culture into binaries whereby each relation is sundered into two diametrically opposed poles – in this case, foundation versus flux, isolation versus interpenetration and essence versus meaninglessness. But in reality, civilisations are characterised by paradoxical dyads rather than binaries. They combine historical continuity with discontinuity. They are resilient insofar as they develop. They go through multiple transmutations, changing shape precisely because they have a certain shape to begin with. Therefore, civilisational identities evolve over time, and civilisations tend to flourish when they interact with one other and when each has a unifying language, which can translate principles into practices that bind its nations and peoples together.

To speak of a distinct and even unique Western civilisation is therefore not to imply any exceptionalism. Rather, recent discoveries in archaeology and anthropology (combined with insights from global history) indicate that the West is like a relational web – a living tradition born of the interactions between the ancient civilisations of Rome, Greece, Babylon, Persia and India, as well as the emergence of Christianity with its roots in Hellenic Judaism.[42] The West emerged first from the Roman encounter with Greco-Babylonian culture and its Persian and Indian influences and later the fusion of Greco-Roman philosophy and law with the biblical legacy. That in turn gave rise to the Europe of Christendom from late Antiquity all the way to the nineteenth century before morphing into the Concert of Europe following the 1815 Vienna Congress and then the Euro-Atlantic community after 1945.[43] Far from being a linear history of progress or a series of absolute breaks, Western civilisation is more like a collection of "family resemblances" (Ludwig Wittgenstein) – all kinds of overlapping similarities without a single core essence.

The liberal civilisation that became hegemonic in the wake of 1989 and is now in crisis contained from the outset the seeds of its own destruction because it posits one single ideology – liberalism – as the West's defining character. Of course, liberal philosophy is diverse and there are many differences between US, English, French and German traditions of liberalism and the various strands of the Enlightenment on which they rest. But binding them together is the primacy of the individual over human association and a conception of liberty as "negative" (freedom of choice without constraints except the law and private conscience). While important differences remain, contemporary liberalism has taken a socially egalitarian, economically individualist and culturally identitarian turn, as I argued in Chapter 2. The liberal emphasis on "negative" freedom rather than substantive, shared ends underpins the promotion of abstract ideals such as emancipation and self-expression that are disembedded from the relationships and institutions, which make human beings political, social animals. And the liberal primacy of the individual over groups has led to the preference for state and market mechanisms over the intermediary institutions of civil society – the free space for human association that is the bedrock of Western civilisation.

The liberal idea of a single civilisation based on universal values has not only inspired the "end of history" thesis but also led to hubris, notably the "Washington consensus" of global capitalism and identity liberalism that are weakening Western cultures and other cultures around the world. At the same time, the Western-dominated liberal world order shows signs of unravelling as a result of divergent interests and values within the Euro-Atlantic community on questions of free trade, immigration and democracy promotion. Whereas the EU is primarily worried by a resurgent and revanchist Russia, the US under President Donald Trump fears most of all China and Islamic fundamentalism. Contemporary liberalism is dividing the West and undermining the civilisational community on which the Western alliance rests. To avoid a further slide into disintegration, Europe and North America need to recover exiled traditions of diplomacy and statecraft that can renew strategic thinking and political action, beginning with a shared sense of purpose based on a common identity rooted in an inherited history and culture. If the West wants to recover its global leadership position, it needs to renew the cultural association of Western nations and peoples in view of a revitalised partnership with other civilisations.

Civic power

Paradoxically, the West as a political community is dominant on the global stage in terms of both soft and hard power, but at the same time, it is undermining its cultural identity and thereby eroding the Western civilisational community from within. Of course, civilisations have always fallen short of their pretention to civility, and the West is no exception – especially when Western elites lecture the rest of the world about the rules of international law and human rights, which they themselves break all-too-often at will. Beyond hypocrisy and double standards (of which all governments and cultures are variously guilty), the West as a liberal civilisation has produced great material achievements, but at the same time, a certain materialism weakens the cultural resources on which they depend – most of all cooperation and trust in institutions. Wealth without a concern for the common good and power without a shared ethical purpose induces complacency, boredom, decadence and a lack of resolve to deal with division, decline and decadence.

At present, Western powers look ill-prepared to defend Western civilisation against internal and external threats. Bereft of belief in its own best traditions, the West has abandoned a generous global outlook and fails to lead by example. The growing backlash against globalisation is amplifying the call to retreat to narrow national self-interest. As the boundaries between wealth and crime are becoming blurred, the West and the world at large now exhibit a general slide into corruption, corporate crime and a disregard for the rule of law from which Western countries are not immune. To retreat to an insular powerlessness in the face of these threats would be to betray Western identity and threaten long-term security and flourishing. The only genuine alternative is to embrace a Burkean vision of the West as something like a commonwealth of nations that reflects a relational covenant among peoples where substantive social and cultural ties based on a common heritage shape identity more than trade or formal treaties.

The many shared traditions that bind together Western cultures across geographic and linguistic boundaries include the Roman idea of citizenship, the Greek notion of a free city, Germanic common law, Jewish and Christian ethics (the dignity of the person, the virtue of free association and the distinction of religious from political authority) and cultural heritage such as Renaissance humanism, the Enlightenment, classicism and Romanticism. In addition, there are collective memories that characterise the Greater West, above all, the shared sacrifice of the two world wars, the fall of the Iron Curtain and more recently the victims from Islamic terrorist attacks.

Renewed Western leadership requires a clear set of objectives and the art of establishing priorities. The first priority is to fight ISIS and radical Islam, which is the single greatest threat to the security of the West. The second priority is to avoid war between the Atlantic West and Russia as well as between US-backed Israel and Saudi Arabia, on the one hand, and Russia-backed Iran and its Shia allies, on the other hand. That has to involve recognising the legacy of civilisational interactions between Rome, Persia and Byzantium – combined with reconciling interests in the Middle East and Eurasia. Key to this is to acknowledge and support the indigenous democratic struggles of the Kurds against Turkey and the Shia in Iraq against both Sunnis and the clerical power in Teheran. The third priority is to transform the international system in a manner that fosters the integration of China and the "rising rest", while avoiding the danger of a "Thucydidean Trap" – a situation in which a conservative status-quo power (the US) confronts a rising new one (China and possibly India).[44] Such a situation could precipitate hostilities in a context where each side lacks a proper cultural understanding of the other and neither has a coherent strategy to avert war.

Paradoxically, just as liberal standards have become globally normative, the West has taken an ultra-liberal turn that undermines the universality of certain Western achievements such as the rule of law, civil liberties and the "mixed constitution" with its balance of power. Western countries have to renew their history of nation- and institution-building both at home and abroad. This means helping to ensure that universal, constitutional provisions and rules are put in place and observed. Otherwise, the continual slide into illiberal rule will accelerate – a tendency that is already on the rise within the liberal West.

Western decline is neither necessary nor normative and entirely avertible because it rests on a cultural pessimism that we owe to the liberal tradition – the triumph of vice over virtue. As the dominant modern political philosophy and ideology, liberalism has sought to remake the West and the wider world in its own image. Western civilisation was not, however, built on the primacy of the individual and on "negative liberty". Instead, the best traditions of the West are based on the dignity of the person and human association around the pursuit of shared ends. These Western ideas and practices grew out of the Roman encounter with Greco-Babylonian culture and its Persian and Indian influences as well as the fusion of Greco-Roman culture with the Judeo-Christian legacy.

Compared with the liberal history of Enlightenment progress that gradually destroyed this inheritance, the alternative conception of Western civilisation that I have briefly sketched connects it to other civilisations and charts a path towards the renewal of the West as a political community that depends for its flourishing on a cultural commonwealth of nations and peoples who covenant with each other – often under religious influence. If the West can renew its civilisational community, its members can overcome their divisions and recover a sense of shared destiny in association with allies and partners in the Western orbit. And if the Greater West can lead once again by example, it might be able to shape the emerging global order more than any other civilisation. In turn, this takes us back to covenant and commonwealth.

Covenant and commonwealth

The liberal world order that is in retreat tends to oscillate between individual states engaged in free trade, on the one hand, and some supranational form of governance, on the other. But this constitutes an inherently unstable balance, which can slide into protectionism, nationalism and war or else technocracy, authoritarianism and a growing gulf between elites and the people they are supposed to represent. The real alternative to either chauvinist nationalism or abstract cosmopolitanism is therefore to re-envision the international order in terms of covenant and commonwealth. The idea of commonwealth as multinational associations of peoples is connected with the notion of covenant – people, often brought together by a shared faith, who are covenanted to one another in the interest of mutual benefit. These modes of association were and still are the heart of international society. Scott Thomas puts this well:

> the global and the local are becoming more closely linked together in a kind of "global particularity". One key example is [...] "globalized Islam", in which types of radical Islam around the world blur the connection between Islam, a specific society, and a specific territory. Another example is the transnational links between churches and denominations that make up global evangelical and Pentecostal

Christianity [...]. These global links or networks do not just happen; they are not free-floating, but are social networks, embedded in religious diaspora communities that are a key aspect of religious transnationalism [...] such social and information networks have been part of much of human history, and a part of the main world religions for centuries, and existed long before the modern international system.⁴⁵

Here one can also cite Martin Wight who wrote that in modernity "[s]overeignty had indeed passed to different states, by social contracts, but the original unity of the human race survived".⁴⁶

An imaginative approach to international affairs by the West would call to abandon false and dysfunctional either/ors in favour of strangely possible paradoxes. Not Pacific or Europe, state or market, religion or secular, or nationalism *versus* globalisation. Instead, intimate reciprocities in ever-widening circles from locality to the whole world can dimly reflect a family of nations and peoples in which states and markets serve the needs of people, communities and associations. Compared with the logic of abstraction that underpins realist, liberal and cosmopolitan ideas, such an "associationist alternative" would link political to economic and ecological purpose in the name of mutuality, reciprocity and social recognition.

Far from being utopian, relational covenants can balance the freedom and dignity of the person with mutual obligations and interpersonal relationships. Against the impersonalism of state and market, covenantal arrangements enable people to partake of both power and wealth in the sense of greater democratic participation and a shared material and spiritual well-being for all. The West can either fracture and split permanently, abandoning international relations to either unipolar hegemony or multipolar anarchy. Or else it can redefine its covenantal destiny – aspiring to be a genuine beacon to the rest of the world and to cooperate with other nations towards the same, shared ends of virtue, honour and mutual flourishing.

Notes

1 Ken Jowitt, 'After Leninism: The New World Disorder', *Journal of Democracy*, Vol. 2, no. 1 (Winter 1991), pp. 11–20, expanded as *The New World Disorder: The Leninist Extinction* (Berkeley, CA: University of California Press, 1992); Stanley Hoffmann, *World Disorders: Troubled Peace in the Post-Cold War Era* (New York: Rowman & Littlefield, 1998).
2 Michael Ignatieff, *Blood and Belonging: Journeys into the New Nationalism* (New York: Farrar, Straus & Giroux, 1994). For a liberal critique of humanitarian interventionism, see David Rieff, *At the Point of a Gun: Democratic Dreams and Armed Intervention* (New York: Simon & Schuster, 2005).

3 Allan Bloom, *The Closing of the American Mind: How Higher Education Has Failed Democracy and Impoverished the Souls of Today's Students* (New York: Simon & Schuster, 1987).

4 On the simultaneous expansion of the capitalist and the black market, see Nils Gilman, Jesse Goldhammer and Steve Weber, *Deviant Globalization. Black Market Economy in the 21st Century* (New York: Continuum, 2011).

5 Francis Fukuyama, 'The End of History?', *The National Interest*, Vol. 16 (Summer 1989), pp. 3–18, expanded as *The End of History and the Last Man* (New York: The Free Press, 1992).

6 Samuel P. Huntington, 'The Clash of Civilizations?', *Foreign Affairs*, Vol. 72, no. 3 (Summer 1993), pp. 22–49, expanded as *The Clash of Civilizations and the Remaking of World Order* (New York: Simon & Schuster 1996).

7 Edward N. Luttwak, 'From Geopolitics to Geo-Economics: Logic of Conflict, Grammar of Commerce', *The National Interest*, Vol. 20 (Summer 1990), pp. 17–23, expanded as *The Endangered American Dream: How to Stop the United States From Being a Third World Country and How to Win the Geo-Economic Struggle for Industrial Supremacy* (New York: Basic Books, 1993).

8 David J. Geanakopolis, *Byzantine East and Latin West: Two Worlds of Christendom in Middle Ages and Renaissance* (Oxford: Blackwell 1966).

9 Jürgen Habermas, *The Divided West* (Oxford: Wiley, 2006).

10 Kwame Anthony Appiah, *Mistaken Identities: Creed, Country, Color, Culture*, 2016 BBC Reith Lectures, at http://downloads.bbc.co.uk/radio4/transcripts/2016_reith4_Appiah_Mistaken_Identities_Culture.pdf; this section draws on an essay entitled 'The Greater West: The Limits of Liberal Civilization and the Renewal of Western Statecraft', in Russell Berman and Kiron Skinner (eds.), *The Future of Western Civilization* (Palo Alto, CA: Stanford University Press, 2019), *forthcoming*.

11 Rémi Brague, *Europe, la voie romaine* (Paris: Folio, 1999); trans. *Eccentric Culture: A Theory of Western Civilization*, tr. Samuel Lester (New York: St. Augustine's Press, 2009).

12 Giles E.M. Gasper, *Anselm of Canterbury and His Theological Inheritance* (Aldershot: Ashgate, 2004), pp. 107–173 and 201–266; Sylvain Gouguenheim, *Aristote au Mont Saint-Michel: Les Racines Grecques de l'Europe Chrétienne* (Paris: Seuil, 2008).

13 Appiah, *Mistaken Identities*, p. 6.

14 *Ibid.*, p. 7.

15 See Francis Oakley, *Natural Law, Laws of Nature, Natural Rights: Continuity and Discontinuity in the History of Ideas* (New York: Continuum, 2005), pp. 87–109; Michel Villey, *La formation de la pensée juridique moderne* (Paris: PUF, 2006); Roger Scruton, *The West and the Rest: Globalisation and the Terrorist Threat* (London: Continuum, 2005); Catherine Pickstock, 'Numbers of Power, Lines of Transition: Metaphysics and the Problem of International Order', *Oxford Journal of Law and Religion*, Vol. 2, no. 1 (2012), pp. 72–97.

16 Appiah, *Mistaken Identities*, p. 8.

17 Niall Ferguson, *Civilization: The West and the Rest* (London: Allen Lane, 2011).

18 Kenneth Clarke, *Civilisation: A Personal View* (London: John Murray, 2005).

19 See Robert Brenner, *Merchants and Revolution: Commercial Change, Political Conflict and London's Overseas Traders 1550–1653* (London: Verso, 2003).

20 Walter Burkert, *Die orientalisierende Epoche in der griechischen Religion und Literatur* (Heidelberg: Carl Winter, 1984); trans. *The Orientalizing Revolution:*

Near Eastern Influences on Greek Culture in the Early Archaic Age, tr. Margaret E. Pinder and Walter Burkert (Cambridge, MA: Harvard University Press, 1992); Jack Goody, *The East in the West* (Cambridge: Cambridge University Press, 1996).

21 Christopher Coker, *The Rise of the Civilizational State* (Cambridge: Polity Press, 2019).

22 See Nicolas Laos, *The Metaphysics of World Order: A Synthesis of Philosophy, Theology, and Politics* (Eugene, OR: Wipf & Stock, 2016); Artur Mrówczynski-Van Allen, Teresa Obolevitch and Paweł Rojek (eds.), *Beyond Modernity: Russian Religious Philosophy and Post-Secularism* (Eugene, OR: Wipf & Stock, 2016).

23 Martin Hengel, 'Das Problem der Hellenisierung Judäas im 1. Jahrhundert nach Christus (under Mitarbeit von Christoph Markschies', in Judaica and Hellenistica (Tübingen: Mohr Siebeck, 1996), pp. 1–90; trans. *The 'Hellenization' of Judea in the First Century after Christ*, tr. John Bowden (London; SCM, 1989).

24 Tom Bissell, *Apostle: Travels Among the Tombs of the Twelve* (London: Faber and Faber, 2016).

25 Peter H. Wilson, *The Holy Roman Empire: A Thousand Years of Europe's History* (London: Penguin, 2017); cf. Felipe Fernandez-Armesto, *Millennium, A History of our last Thousand Years* (London: Bantam Press, 1995).

26 Aldo Schiavone, *La storia spezzata. Roma antica e occidente moderno* (Roma-Bari: Laterza, 1996); trans. *The End of the Past: Ancient Rome and the Modern West*, tr. Margery J. Schneider (Cambridge, MA: Harvard University Press, 2002).

27 Charles Taylor, 'What Was the Axial Revolution?', in Robert Bellah and Hans Joas (eds.), *The Axial Age and Its Consequences* (Cambridge: The Belknap Press of Harvard University, 2011), pp. 30–46.

28 Goody, *The East in the West*, p. 250.

29 Joseph Needham, *Science and Civilisation: Introductory Orientations* (Cambridge: Cambridge University Press, 1954).

30 Walter Scheidel (ed.), *Rome and China: Comparative Perspectives on Ancient World Empires* (Oxford: Oxford University Press, 2009).

31 Ian Morris, *Why the West Rules for Now. The Patterns of History and What They Reveal About the Future* (London: Profile Books, 2010), p. 271.

32 Peter Frankopan, *The Silk Roads: A New History of the World* (London: Bloomsbury, 2015).

33 Felipe Fernandez-Armesto, *The World: A History* (Boston: Prentice Hall, 2011).

34 Robert D. Kaplan, *The Revenge of Geography: What the Map Tells us About Coming Conflicts and the Battle Against Fate* (New York: Random House, 2012).

35 Harold J. Mackinder, 'The Geographical Pivot of History', *The Geographical Society*, Vol. 23, no. 4 (1904), pp. 421–437; *Democratic Ideals and Reality. A Study in the Politics of Reconstruction* (New York: Holt 1919).

36 Mackinder, *Democratic Ideals and Reality*, p. 150.

37 Oswald Spengler, *Der Untergang des Abendlandes – Umrisse einer Morphologie der Weltgeschichte* (Wien: Braumüller, 1918); trans. *The Decline of the West*, Arthur Helps and Helmut Werner (eds.); tr. Charles F. Atkinson (New York: Oxford University Press, 1991).

38 Pierre Manent, *Les métamorphoses de la cité. Essai sur la dynamique de l'Occident* (Paris: Flammarion, 2010); trans. *Metamorphoses of the City.*

On the Western Dynamic, tr. Marc LePain (Cambridge, MA: Harvard University Press, 2013).

39 Oliver Stuenkel, *Post-Western World: How Emerging Powers are Remaking Global* Order (Cambridge: Polity Press, 2016).

40 I have argued this in greater detail in a forthcoming essay entitled 'The Greater West: The Limits of Liberal Civilization and the Renewal of Western Statecraft', in Russell Berman and Kiron Skinner (eds.), *The Future of Western Civilization* (Palo Alto, CA: Stanford University Press, 2019), on which this chapter builds.

41 These three assumptions are myths that I have adapted from Christopher Coker's *The Rise of the Civilizational-State*.

42 Walter Burkert, *The Orientalizing Revolution: Near Eastern Influences on Greek Culture in the Early Archaic Age*, tr. Margaret E. Pinder and Walter Burkert (Cambridge, MA: Harvard University Press, 1992); Jack Goody, *The East in the West* (Cambridge: Cambridge University Press, 1996).

43 Peter H. Wilson, *The Holy Roman Empire: A Thousand Years of Europe's History* (London: Penguin, 2017).

44 Christopher Coker, *The Improbable War: China, the United States and the Logic of Great Power Conflict* (London: Hurst, 2014).

45 Scott M. Thomas, 'Religions and Global Security', *Quaderni di Relazioni Internazionali*, Vol. 12, no. 2 (2010), pp. 4–21 (quotes at pp. 10, 12).

46 Martin Wight, *International Theory: The Three Traditions*, Gabriele Wight and Brian Porter (eds.) (Leicester: Leicester University Press, 1991), p. 38.

Conclusion
The once and future order

The liberal world order is not limited to the international organisations that form the system of global governance. It rests on the ideology and philosophy of liberalism, which in the final analysis threatens to collapse back into the materialism that is one half of its dualist worldview, evacuating the ungrounded idealism that is its other half. Starting in the nineteenth century, liberalism tended towards a procedural formalism and a cultural vacuity, which were challenged by the materialist philosophies of Nazism, Fascism and Communism that sought to re-construct positive liberty on a non-religious, supposedly scientific basis. And following their eventual collapse in the twentieth century, liberalism has insisted on its own latent materialism. Not only has the soul disappeared, but also the subject and along with it the citizen and ultimately the idea of humans as social and creative beings.

Where the new fascists in the West and elsewhere pander to the politics of fear and exclusion of the alien (immigrant or refugee), mainstream politics needs to develop a politics of hope and meaning, which addresses popular concerns about loss and insecurity, and offers a positive vision of patriotism and international solidarity. A Burkean vision of association promotes individual fulfilment and mutual flourishing, though always mediated by local inheritances and specificities. Nor could resurgent nationalism and new forms of racism stand in greater contrast to it. Not only is neo-fascism chauvinist and immoral, but it is also nostalgic because it seeks an exaggerated version of recent modernity.

So the worldwide revulsion against liberalism is a sign that we have entered new times. Yet Brexit, Trump, other anti-establishment insurgencies in the West and the authoritarian regimes of the illiberal non-West are profoundly ambivalent insofar as they do not simply push back against global market fundamentalism and progressive social engineering. They also fuse anti-liberal with ultra-liberal ideas. Some insurgents and non-Western autocrats want to undo socially liberal reforms, such as abortion or certain minority rights, while cracking down on immigrants in a raging fit of atavistic ethnocentrism. There is also an ultra-liberal creed at work in the worship of the Hobbesian sovereign state and the invocation of "The People" in ways that are neo-totalitarian. Connecting anti-liberal with ultra-liberal ideas is a cult of mere will, which is unmediated by civic institutions or highbrow cultural traditions – a kind of will-to-power in a novel guise.

There remains a clear need for a broad popular movement in shaping a politics of the common good – a movement that can overcome the binaries that divides Western countries and increasingly the whole world: young *versus* old, owners *versus* workers, natives *versus* immigrants, city *versus* countryside, faithful *versus* secular. Instead, resistance must be based on the primacy of positive liberty and a substantive vision of true human flourishing.

Therefore, any viable alternative has to focus on cultural identities, but reach for ones more linked to noble aspirations than to fearful prejudice. A plausible, constructive alternative to the liberal world order is about discerning the positive goals that human beings can share in common and which alone allow them real flourishing and a deeper freedom. Instead of rewarding vice (as in liberalism), we need to renew institutions that encourage virtue. In increasingly heterogeneous societies, greater social and cultural cohesion requires a plural search for the common good. The new politics of belonging that liberals have neglected requires a positive conception of identity, combining civic patriotism with an internationalist outlook. By replacing liberal value moralism with virtues of humility, generosity, loyalty and fraternity, we can renew statecraft and diplomacy in a quest to build a more equitable world order. Above all this requires courage, which is missing among leaders in the West and beyond. As Alexander Solzhenitsyn's prescient remarks in 1978 suggest,

> A decline in courage may be the most striking feature, which an outside observer notices in the West in our days. The Western world has lost its civil courage, both as a whole and separately, in each country, each government, each political party, and, of course, in the United Nations. Such a decline in courage is particularly noticeable among the ruling groups and the intellectual elite, causing an impression of loss of courage by the entire society. Of course, there are many courageous individuals, but they have no determining influence on public life.[1]

For these reasons, this essay has sought to renew and develop the legacy of Edmund Burke. Far from moralising, Burke thought human beings capable of both vice and virtue. The role of politics is to limit as much as possible the vices of greed and selfishness. It is also to encourage social virtues of generosity, loyalty and duty that nurture the way we live in society.

Appeals to the abstract ideals of *liberté* and *égalité* ring hollow. They overlook the relationships with our family, friends or fellow citizens, which provide substance to otherwise vacuous values.

Burke rejected the possessive individualism of liberal thinking in favour of social freedom. True liberty is secured by what he called "equality of restraint", not empty free choice. Freedom and equality require lived fraternity among citizens who have common needs. But the dominant political traditions have abandoned any sense of interpersonal solidarity. They have instead embraced the impersonal forces of collective state control and atomised market exchange that undermines society.

His emphasis on covenantal ties among generations can help us think through the growing economic injustice between young and old today. Society is not a contract of individuals. It is a partnership between the living, the dead and those yet to be born. This conception balances individual rights with mutual obligations and contributions with rewards. Covenants endow social relations with meaning that is missing from Hobbes' and Locke's idea of a social contract because it ignores our social nature. Human beings are not atomised agents maximising their utility. And they are not anonymous carriers of historical laws. We are born into social relations, "the little platoon we belong to in society", and these are the first object of our affections. We learn to love and care for family, neighbours and friends. This love creates a sense of attachment and belonging that extends to our fellow citizens and humankind – the strangers in our midst who become part of our communities.

Liberalism and its illiberal enemies have little to say about our social nature. We are embodied beings who are embedded in relationships and institutions. They command affection and forge attachment as they are rooted in people's identity and interests. These "public affections", as Burke terms them, are indispensable to the good functioning of the rule of law. They build trust and cooperation on which a prosperous market economy and a vibrant democracy depend. His appeal to love and affection reflects the primacy of relationships over impersonal mechanisms. The practice of lived fraternity can shape a politics of affection and attachment to people, place and purpose.

This primacy of real relationships extends from the domestic arena to international relations. The strongest partnerships nations forge come not through treaties or trade but through cultural association. These social bonds take generations to develop. The UK post-Brexit risks tearing up the fabric of mutual ties with her continental European partners by privileging a free trade deal over cultural exchange and influence. In the wider Europe (including Russia), people are connected across different cultures through shared customs and habits of life. This is true of nations as much as of individuals. These customs involve high cultural traditions of philosophy, literature and the arts. They also include popular culture that is reflected in food, music, clothes, architecture and the folk tales of Tolkien or the Brothers Grimm. National identities differ, but Europeans have more in common than divides them.

Europe, like other civilisations, is what Burke called a "commonwealth of cultures" – an association of nations and peoples with a shared history and destiny. Today, social exchange and a common cultural inheritance are as necessary to promote peace and partnerships as political diplomacy or the use of military force. After Brexit and Trump, the West faces a stark choice. It can either pursue global free trade that will reinforce economic and social discontent at home. Or it can help to build a new cultural alliance spanning the US, Europe and the countries of the Commonwealth.

Burke is often portrayed as an apologist of empire, but that ignores his fight against American and Irish oppression and the exploitation of India. International politics has to involve a search for shared interest based on what he referred to as "our common humanity". On that basis, he condemned sectarianism at home and colonial injustice abroad. His admiration for the Indians as "a people for ages civilised and cultivated" outflanked in advance the imperial nostalgia of Boris Johnson and his fellow Tory Brexiteers. It also rejects the "clash of civilisations" prophecy so beloved by senior members of the Trump administration. Building commonwealths of culture is one of the international routes not yet taken and Burke's political thought remains a rich resource for a new approach. Politics is about nurturing a sense of fraternity both at home and abroad. A middle path of courage and prudence can renew the once and future order of human association.

Note

1   Alexander Solzhenitsyn, Harvard University, 8 June 1978.

Index

For Product Safety Concerns and Information please contact our EU
representative GPSR@taylorandfrancis.com
Taylor & Francis Verlag GmbH, Kaufingerstraße 24, 80331 München, Germany

www.ingramcontent.com/pod-product-compliance
Lightning Source LLC
Chambersburg PA
CBHW050537270326
41926CB00015B/3273